R Fran[...]

7 Dec 73

U. S.

Lake Balkhash

Tashkent

Alma Ata

Urumchi

ALTAI MOUNTAINS

MONGOLIAN

TIEN SHAN

Kashgar

TARIM BASIN

SINKIANG UIGHUR
AUTONOMOUS REGION

Lop Nor

HINDU KUSH

AFGHAN-
ISTAN

Kabul

Indus R.

PAMIRS

KUN LUN MTS.

Yumen

KANSU

PAKISTAN

TSINGHAI

Koko Nor

Lu Chia

Lanchow

Gartok

PEOPLE'S

REPUBLIC

OF

PLATEAU OF TIBET

TIBETAN
AUTONOMOUS REGION

New Delhi

NEPAL

Lhasa

SZECHWAN

Chengtu

Katmandu

Everest

Brahmaputra R.

Ganges R.

SIKKIM

BHUTAN

ASSAM

Yangtze R.

INDIA

BANGLA-
DESH

Calcutta

Dacca

Irrawaddy R.

YUNNAN

Kunming

BURMA

Mekong

BAY OF BENGAL

Hanoi

PEOPLE'S REPUBLIC OF
CHINA
AND ADJACENT COUNTRIES

+—+—+ Railroads
——— Auto roads in outlying
areas

A.R. Autonomous Region
⤙ Dams

0   MILES   500

LAOS

Vientiane

Rangoon

THAILAND

Bangkok

P. TREMBLAY

THE LONG
REVOLUTION

THE LONG REVOLUTION

★

Edgar Snow

Vintage Books
A Division of Random House
New York

FIRST VINTAGE BOOKS EDITION, August 1973

Library of Congress Cataloging in Publication Data
Snow, Edgar, 1905–1972.
The long revolution.
1. China—Description and travel—1949–
I. Title.
[DS711.S57   1973]   951.05   73-4517
ISBN 0-394-71930-1

Portions of this manuscript have been published, in a different form, in *Life* and in *The New Republic*.

Manufactured in the United States of America

Acknowledgments

I am deeply grateful to Mary Heathcote, who has worked with my husband as an editor and a friend for many years. She was with him in Switzerland during the writing of this book and continued her work on the manuscript in New York after his death.

I am also grateful to our good friend O. Edmund Clubb, who read the manuscript with the care and attention he previously gave to my husband's other books.

A special note of thanks to Jean Pohoryles, who has somehow bridged time and distance gaps to coordinate the whole.

L.W.S.

Publisher's Note

Edgar Snow returned from his last trip to China in February of 1971. He died on February 15, 1972. Had he lived, he would undoubtedly have added documentation in the manner of his notes and bibliographies for the new editions of *Red Star Over China* and *Red China Today: The Other Side of the River*. He would certainly have augmented from his notes the accounts of his 1970-71 interviews with Chairman Mao Tse-tung and Premier Chou En-lai.

Edgar Snow's wife, Lois Wheeler Snow, wrote in her letter giving consent to publication of *The Long Revolution,* "The book is an unfinished work—a beginning punctuated by the abrupt ending that death decreed for my husband. In it are the seeds of a new relationship between the people of China and America. If we nourish them they will grow."

Contents

Photographs following pages 82–83, 178–179
(All photographs not otherwise credited were
taken by the author)

Part One

A Different Country?

I

Encounter
at T'ien An Men

It was a perfect October day in Peking for the twenty-first anniversary celebration of the founding of the People's Republic. Seated unsuspectingly on the crowded balcony of T'ien An Men (Heavenly Peace Gate), I felt a tug at my sleeve and turned to see Premier Chou En-lai there. He quickly led me and my wife, Lois, to stand beside Chairman Mao, where for some minutes we occupied positions at the center of China's one fourth (or is it one fifth?) of mankind. Nothing the Chinese leaders publicly do is without purpose. Something significant was happening, but what was it?

Across the wide square, which holds half a million people, a large signboard proclaimed, in letters readable a block away, an excerpt from Mao Tse-tung's statement of May 20, 1970. The occasion then was the declaration of China's firm support for Prince Sihanouk's resistance to the Lon Nol coup d'état and to Lon Nol's American allies in Cambodia, and for the newly formed anti-American alliance of the Indochinese peoples. To emphasize the point, Prince Sihanouk stood there too, on the other side of the Chairman. The Prince was smiling—he likes to smile—and to my wife's remark that we were not the only

Americans who opposed the Cambodian invasion he proffered a warm reply, "The American people are our friends!"

"Peoples of the world," read Mao's summons, "unite to defeat the U.S. aggressors and all their running dogs [*tsou-kou*]!"

In Chinese propaganda clichés, running dogs means servile accomplices.

When our balcony photograph was later published by the *People's Daily* on the Chairman's seventy-seventh birthday I was described as a "friendly American." In the upper right-hand corner, which contains the Mao Thought for the day, was a box which enclosed the words, "Peoples of the world, including the American people, are all our friends."

Chairman Mao takes pains to separate people from governments and their policies. If a symbol was needed for that, I was pleased to be it: that is, to represent the many Americans against the armed invasion and destruction of Vietnam and other Indochinese countries. Was I there to receive a salute to the war resisters in the United States who were at last bringing a halt to what General Matthew Ridgway had prophetically called a "tragic blunder"? Yes, it was that—but something more, too. . . .

Foreign press canards had described Mao's hand as palsied and kept hidden in his sleeve but I noticed that his handshake was as firm as ever. He had lost some extra weight and looked fitter than when I had last seen him in 1965—at a moment, I now realized, when he had been making perhaps the most crucial and daring decision of his life as a revolutionary leader. That decision was to purge his Party-chosen successor, Liu Shao-ch'i, vice-chairman of the Communist Party and chairman of the Republic, along with other Party members "in authority who are taking the capitalist road"—and all *their* running dogs— targets of the Great Proletarian Cultural Revolution.

Mao spoke about it briefly as we watched the ingenious floats and *tableaux vivants* roll past. What organization! And what color and variety of costume in contrast to drab everyday clothes worn by workers and intellectuals alike. Most of China's minority nationalities were there, some forty-seven of them, who speak over twenty different languages and make up 5 or 6 percent of the total population—now between 750 and 800 million. The day's theme was production and preparedness: blue and gray uniforms were everywhere but one saw few weapons except in the hands of teenage militia, including girls with their hair in pony tails.

Each tableau exceeded the other in glorification of Mao's works, maxims, and directives, as followed in commune, factory, cultural, and military life. Most spectacular: a range of mountains pierced by tunnels joined by bridges supporting a rapidly moving model train represented completion of the last link in a rail system which now joined farthest Chinese Turkestan with the southern frontier at Vietnam. Never out of sight were statues and busts, some of great size, which reproduced the erect figure beside me, leader and initiator of the second or cultural liberation, aimed to restore the purity of the revolution and involve the masses in its direction as never before. *"Mao Chuhsi wansui! Mao Chuhsi wansui wansui! Mao Chuhsi wansui wansui wansui!"* "Chairman Mao, ten thousand times ten thousand times ten thousand years!" rang the chorus below, where tears sprang to many eyes, and not only among the young.

"How does it look to you?" I could not resist asking, as I waved toward the adoring marchers. "How does it *feel?*"

Mao grimaced, shook his head, and said that it was better but he was not satisfied. In what way? Before he could reply we were interrupted by new arrivals. Only some weeks later, in a lengthy talk, was I able to repeat the question—and then he spoke quite frankly about the "nuisance" of the personality cult. But I discovered that on that October day his mind had not been on the images and flags and flowers with which human hands and heads animated Mao quotations. He was thinking about the problems of rebuilding the Party and the state superstructure, about recovering the rhythm of production lost during the cultural upheaval, about hastening the end of the Vietnamese war, and about widening China's contacts with the outside world. Was he also thinking about a possible dialogue with Richard Nixon?

We were having a rebellion of sorts in the United States now, were we not? he asked me. He was impressed by the American war-resistance movement—which he had applauded in that May 20 statement—and he wanted to hear more about its political meaning. We would, he said, soon meet again.

2

A Hint from Premier Chou

I had lived and worked in China during the first
Nationalist-Communist civil war and during part of the
Second World War.[1] Finally in 1960 I was able to return,
as again in 1964-65 and now in 1970. Lois Wheeler, my
actress wife, had never been to China before, although
she had been offered a visa with me. On earlier occasions,
however, our U.S. State Department had refused to
"validate" her passport for travel in China, held to be
"not in the national interest." This time she came without
waiting for Washington's permission.

My own 1960 and 1965 "validations" had been yielded
only after pressure applied at a high level in Washington
by my publishers. At the same level my subsequent
reports had of course been ignored. But that story of a
decade of lost effort to penetrate the lofty realms of
policy making with a few pieces of useful information—
and the chance to "begin anew with China," as John
Kennedy put it in his inaugural speech in 1963 and
quickly forgot, instead to take his presidential turn at
entrapping us in the Vietnam jungles—has been told
elsewhere.[2]

[1] As a correspondent: see *Journey to the Beginning* (Random
House, New York, 1957; Vintage Books, 1972).

[2] See *Red China Today: The Other Side of the River* (Random
House, New York, 1962; Vintage Books, 1971).

Now here was Lois by my side, and among the very few American women ever to enter the People's Republic, with a pair of alert and receptive brown eyes to help my own. We reached Peking in early August, entering what Pekingese call the Tiger Heat—mitigated somewhat nowadays by the shade of myriad trees and neighboring afforestation.

Hardly any foreigners, even among old-time resident sympathizers, had been permitted to travel outside Peking since early in the cultural revolution.[3] Formerly routine tourist sights—the Great Wall, the Ming Tombs, the Western Hills, even the grand museums and palaces of Peking—had been closed to visitors. When I began to retrace old paths to such places with Lois, diplomats and foreign residents were encouraged to hope—and they were right—that the "worst of the tension" was about over.

We spent a whole week at two universities I used to know well—Yenching, where I once lectured, and nearby Tsing Hua, a noted engineering school. There we heard first-hand accounts of the years of cultural combat and the university upheaval, with the Red Guard story and its sequels. We saw modern and rural hospitals, a locomotive plant, a steel mill, and heard other sides of the cultural revolution. We flew to Shensi province, in the Northwest, and from its capital, Sian, went on to Yenan, the celebrated wartime guerrilla capital. Westward then to Pao An (Tze Dan)—the first foreigners to go there since 1945—and deep into the hills where in 1936 I first met Mao Tse-tung, then a hunted "Red bandit."[4] We saw a state farm run by the army and a political reform school

[3] One exception was my oldest foreign friend in China, the New Zealander Rewi Alley, who is possibly the most traveled man in Chinese history. He is soon bringing out a book devoted to his travels during the cultural revolution.

[4] See *Red Star Over China* (Random House, New York, 1937; rev. ed., Grove Press, New York, 1968, 1971).

where a former Sian Party Committee chairman showed us the piggeries of which he was now in charge. And back to Sian and Peking, and lots of theater and lots of talk with old friends over good food, and then on to the Northeast, above the Great Wall. More industry, a deaf-mute school run by army acupuncturists, the great Anshan steel complex—and then far down south to see the Trade Fair at Canton. Up again to the east coast and tea-planted Chekiang, on to Shanghai and the Lower Yangtze, and more communes and friendly people.

Altogether, I visited eleven communes in six months before I left China in February, making a total of thirty-three communes—at all points of the Chinese compass—where I have been welcomed during the past decade. Now everywhere the land lay green, more leveled off, better terraced, thickly tree-planted, and nearer the garden state Mao promised years ago. And everywhere we provoked crowds startled at the vision of the first Occidentals seen for years. That was, of course, still a few months Before Ping-Pong.

And ping-pong was where I was first welcomed back by Premier Chou En-lai.

It was August 18, 1970. We had been invited to a table-tennis match between North Korean and Chinese teams but had declined owing to a previous dinner engagement. In the midst of some roast duck my friend Yao Wei (with whom I had shared many earlier adventures[5]) phoned to say, simply, "Get ready for a trip." That meant a command appearance: I guessed it might be from the Premier, and so it was. We found him at the Table Tennis Stadium—a beautiful new building which seats 18,000—presiding at the match with octogenarian Vice-Chairman (of the People's Republic) Tung Pi-wu, Prince Sihanouk and his charming consort, chief of the army general staff Huang Yung-sheng, Vice-

[5] See *Red China Today, op. cit.*

Chairman Li Hsien-nien, and a host of other notables.

Soon after our arrival Premier Chou left his seat and shortly afterward I was called down to one of the reception rooms, where he awaited me. As nimble-witted as ever, his hair faintly beginning to silver, wearing a summer sport shirt and gray slacks above sandals and white socks, the seventy-two-year-old Chou greeted me cordially, discussed my travel plans, and soon got into politics. (Messengers kept bringing him game scores, so that he could be on hand for the finish. These tourneys are climaxed when Chinese leaders and their guests go down to the floor to shake hands and congratulate and be photographed with the teams.)

The Premier asked many questions about the United States, which led me to wonder whether he thought our domestic economic and political problems were so critical now as to "rule out new major American military initiatives in Asia." He handed that one back to me to answer myself but reminded me that China had a second threat on the north—a million Soviet troops mobilized along the frontiers.

"If China sought a détente," I asked, "would the possibilities be better for negotiating with Russia or the United States?"

"I've been asking myself the same question," he replied.

Ping-pong scores having now arrived to indicate that the matches were ending, the Premier said we would talk about my last question at our next meeting. We finished our coffee and went up to shake hands with the winners and losers.

I saw the Premier briefly on October 1, when he said that the Americans had proposed reopening Sino-American talks but that China was not interested. Later that month I left some questions with him, and on November 5, after my return to Peking, he granted me four hours of mixed conversation and interview in the impressive Fukien Room of the Great Hall of the People. The Premier as usual had important things to say—but his most arresting remarks concerned a possible Sino-American meeting in Peking.

As for China's terms, they still began with a demand that the United States take its arms and ships away from the island of Taiwan (Formosa).[6] In 1960 Chairman Mao had permitted me to quote directly only a few sentences from our talk, but among them were: "We want to maintain world peace. We do not want war. We hold that war should not be used as a means to settle disputes between nations. However, not only China but the United States, as well, has the responsibility to maintain peace." He added, *"Taiwan is China's affair. We will insist on this."*

Now, Chou repeated what he too had spelled out for me in 1960 and 1965. "Taiwan is China's internal affair" (and must be settled by the Chinese themselves). "United States armed aggression there is another question, an international question, and we are ready to negotiate *that*," said Chou.

He now added some news. He recalled that when President Nixon came to office in 1969 he had announced that he favored relaxation of tension and wanted to negotiate with China. Further, *Nixon had informed Peking that, if Warsaw was not an appropriate place, discussions could be held in China. Peking had replied, That's fine. Nixon could come there himself or send an emissary to discuss the Taiwan question.*

There was no response from Nixon, however. Then came the Cambodian invasion of March, 1970. The

[6] Chinese territory seized by Japan in the war of 1895 and promised to China at the Cairo (1943) and Potsdam (1945) conferences. Taiwan province became Chiang Kai-shek's sanctuary when he fled from the mainland revolution in 1949. Truman put a naval blockade around Taiwan in 1950, thus intervening to prevent unification. In 1955 Eisenhower formalized the *de facto* American protectorate in an alliance with Chiang—while the United States recognized and financed Chiang's Nationalist government as the pretended sovereign over all China, keeping Chiang seated in the United Nations and the People's Republic out of it until 1971.

Chinese concluded that Nixon was not to be taken seriously.

"Is the door still open?" I asked.

"The door is open but it depends on whether the United States is serious in dealing with the Taiwan question." All other matters, he added, were "branch questions" as between Peking and Washington.

That was the end of that bit of colloquy. From other comments it was evident to me that the Chinese saw Nixon's "peace initiative" as a ruse. They closely watched not only his maneuvers in Southeast Asia but also moves to build up Japanese military power in a receivership to take over advanced American "defense positions" in East Asia, as well as gambits for a possible deal with Russia at China's expense.

The Premier had spoken freely and it was not always clear where interview ended and conversation not then publishable began. I submitted for correction a long dispatch based on my notes. It was a week before clearance came. The official version omitted all references to the words italicized above. Within that week President Yahya Khan had arrived from Pakistan. As is now well known, he brought with him a personal letter from President Nixon which formally raised the question of his visit to Peking, preceded by an emissary (Mr. Henry Kissinger) authorized "to discuss the Taiwan question."

Within a few more weeks I was to learn, from Chairman Mao, that Nixon's emissary might soon be on his way.

I asked myself why I had been entrusted with such knowledge. I remembered that in 1936 I had carried with me, and retained when I secretly entered and left the Red bases in Northwest China, the knowledge that Chiang Kai-shek's deputy commander-in-chief, Chang Hsueh-liang, had reached a secret agreement with the Reds to cooperate with them to force his chief to end the civil war and form a united front to oppose Japan. There was a good reason then, too, why I should have that information.

3

Essence of
the Cultural Revolution

I have referred to Chairman Mao's preoccupation with
the problem of rebuilding the Party and the state superstructure. Why should they need rebuilding? That short
question requires long answers, touched upon later, but
here it may be useful to suggest a few reasons for the
Great Proletarian Cultural Revolution, which had the
effect of temporarily dissolving the Chinese Communist
Party, if not the government itself.

The extensive purge began in mid-1966, led by Mao,
and lasted till April, 1969, when the Ninth Party Congress
elected a new Central Committee composed of a nucleus
of surviving protoplasm reinforced by "new blood." In
November, 1970, Chou En-lai told me that something like
95 percent of the former Party members[1] had by then
been reinstated. Reinstated, but not necessarily reassigned;
many awaited "liberation" following completion of
"struggle-criticism-transformation," the three-stage formula
for redemption.

One of Mao's aims was to "simplify the administrative

[1] Early in 1966 Party members were said to number about twenty
million and 80 percent of them were post-1949 recruits.

structure" and "eliminate duplication." At provincial and urban centers I found the reductions drastic enough, but in the capital the skeletizing of the central government superstructure was especially severe. Early in 1971 Premier Chou told me that he was assisted by only two vice-premiers, for example, whereas formerly there were seven.

"In the past there were ninety departments directly under the central government," he said. "Now there will be only twenty-six. They are all run at present by revolutionary committees, and in each committee the Party nucleus is the core of the leadership. Formerly there were more than 60,000 administrative personnel in the central government. Now it is about 10,000."

Where had the displaced cadres gone? About 80 percent of those from Peking were sent to rural centers known as May Seventh schools,[2] a term deriving from a Mao Tse-tung directive of that date, in 1968. In such schools reeducation in socialism and Mao Tse-tung Thought was combined with self-supporting labor on commune farms, often working newly opened land. "Going down" to commune schools was not just punishment but said to be regarded as continuing reeducation in the Party. In the future *all* but the highest cadres would periodically be "sent down" to undergo ideological checkups as a kind of routine political therapy.

"The ablest of the exurbanite cadres will go or have already gone to strengthen leadership in various [provincial] localities," said Chou. "Many are needed to help run industries and institutes formerly under central government ministries but now being turned over to local management. Among others, many were past sixty and ready for retirement on pension. Some will choose to live with their families in the communes." There would be work for all.

[2] See Chapter 17, Alice in Nanniwan.

Such decentralization policies also reflected intensified regional and local self-sufficiency aims not only in food but in industrialization, based partly on growing rural electric power. There continued to be organized migrations, on a massive scale, of educated urban youths and adults for new employment into the interior county cities and communes. In Shanghai alone the exodus since 1965 approached one million. Estimates of the total, including many from the student Red Guard detachments who first launched the cultural revolution, ran into many millions of migrants.

But such reforms in the superstructure were only one aspect of the national *bouleversement*. Mao's basic aim was no less than to proletarianize Party thinking and, beyond that, to push the proletariat really to take power for themselves, and in the process to create a new culture free of domination by the feudal and bourgeois heritage.

It was for no less than that end that Mao Tse-tung deliberately risked wrecking the Party which he, more than anyone else, had built. At the start Mao's intention was to remove "only a handful" from power. In its sweeping reach the hand gathered in many senior veteran leaders and some of Mao's oldest comrades. Above all, they included Liu Shao-ch'i, who in 1959 had succeeded Mao as titular head of state. Why and how did that happen?

Mao had been effective head of the Party since 1935 and official Party chairman since 1943 when, in 1956, Liu became Mao's first deputy. But by 1964 Mao had lost effective control over much of the Party hierarchy set up by his "successors," and over the state administrative apparatus also. In 1965 Mao could not get the Party-controlled press in Peking to publish a highly important document meant to launch the propaganda stage of the Great Proletarian Cultural Revolution—so he told me in 1970. He had to have it published in pamphlet form in Shanghai. The "important document" was a long critique of a play by Wu Han entitled *Hai Jui Dismissed from*

Office,[3] an allegorical attack on Mao Tse-tung for having secured the removal of Defense Minister P'eng Teh-huai and his replacement by Lin Piao at a Party plenary session held in Lushan in 1959. Liu Shao-ch'i, P'eng Chen, the mayor of Peking, Lu Ting-yi, chief of the Party Propaganda Department, and Chou Yang, Lu's deputy, were among those who opposed publication.

It was Liu Shao-ch'i and his allies in the Central Committee who ran the superstructure, the labor unions, the Party schools, the Communist Youth Leagues, the millions of Party cadres and bureaucrats, all in Mao's name. Probably most cadres considered themselves loyal Maoists. It seemed that Liu and his like-minded comrades were, especially after the economic crisis of 1959-61, tolerating the Mao cult in theory and slighting Mao Thought in performance. They tended to put economics before man, encourage effort by material incentives first and zeal second, push production without class struggle, boost technology by relying on "experts," put economics in command of politics to serve technology, and favor the city over the countryside. They wanted expansion of state credit (and state debt) rather than Great Leaps Forward and ideological faith in building capital by hard collective labor.

Such were the allegations brought forth by the cultural revolution.

The crisis between Mao and Liu had been building up even before the clash over the choice of Lin Piao to replace P'eng Teh-huai, in 1959. That was Mao's first overt move in a struggle he foresaw with the growingly powerful urban-based bureaucracy headed by Liu. Lin Piao was Mao's most faithful army disciple, and vice-chairman of the Party Military Affairs Commission, of which Mao had retained chairmanship ever since 1935. Though Liu might be head of state and control the nonmilitary cadres,

---

[3] See Chapter 12, Conspiracy by Propaganda.

even while Mao remained Party chairman, the People's Liberation Army was the trump card in any showdown. With Lin Piao in command that card seemed secure in Mao's hand. But Mao let events determine the outcome, and apparently did not finally give up hope of winning Liu around to initiate the purge of his own followers until much later than many supposed.

"When did you finally decide that Liu had to go?" I asked him during our conversation in December of 1970.

He replied that the moment of decision came in January, 1965. At that time he had put before the Politburo a program for the coming cultural revolution. That program was an outgrowth of the Socialist Education Movement,[4] which was carried out first of all in the army under Lin Piao's direction, spread into the rural communes, and then had faltered in the cities. The first point of the Socialist Education program had specifically denounced and demanded the removal of "those in the Party in authority who are taking the capitalist road." Now it was to be the first point of the new drive, the cultural revolution. Liu had strenuously opposed that first point right at the meeting, said Mao.

"Was it then in January, 1965, the month when I last saw you, that the decision was made to launch the cultural revolution?"

The Chairman said that after October, 1965, when the criticism and repudiation of *Hai Jui Dismissed from Office* was made, things had unfolded rapidly.

The Politburo had earlier (1964) set up a Cultural Revolution Group headed by P'eng Chen, mayor of Peking, secretary of the powerful Peking Party Committee, and protector of Wu Han. In February, 1966, P'eng had sought to shield Wu Han and other writers who had been publishing allegorical attacks on Mao and Maoism. P'eng Chen sought to have their works criticized in terms of

[4] See page 84.

"academic" errors only, not political ones. P'eng had not consulted other members of his committee, nor Mao himself. He was definitely repudiated on May 16, 1966.

On that date, said Mao, an enlarged session of the Politburo met to draw up the strategy of the Great Proletarian Cultural Revolution. In August, 1966, the Eleventh Plenary Session of the Central Committee convened and adopted the sixteen-point program[5] of the revolution and its accompanying purge.

"Did Liu Shao-ch'i oppose the sixteen-point decision?" I asked.

He was very ambiguous about it at the plenary session, Mao said, but actually was dead against it. By that time he (Mao) had already put up his *ta tzu-pao*, or big-character poster.[6] Liu was thrown into consternation.

"That was your poster, 'Bombard the Headquarters'? And Liu knew that *he* was Headquarters?"

Yes, at that time the power of the Party, the power over propaganda work, the power of the provincial and local Party committees, power even over the Peking Party Committee, was out of Mao's control. That was why he had said (to me, in January, 1965[7]) that there was no "worship of the individual"—personality cult—to speak of, as yet, but that there was need for it.

Mao frankly began to invoke his enormous personal prestige and popularity, using it as a major weapon in his struggle to recover full authority over the orientation of revolutionary power.

---

[5] For complete text see Appendix, Resolutions of the Eleventh Plenum of the Central Committee—The Sixteen-Point Program.

[6] Large sheets of paper with slogans or messages written by the people and especially by students, pasted on walls, trees, over any conspicuous place available, became an important means of communication used by Red Guards and others to attack Party leaders and the press which denied them publication.

[7] For complete text of the interview, see Appendix, South of the Mountains to North of the Seas.

Now there was, in 1970, no such need, and the "cult" would be *cooled down*, he said. His justification was the need to inspire the whole nation with the élan and the ideals of the Yenan period (1937-47), when Mao had written his principal works, and when his leadership had prepared revolutionary followers for final victory.

Now it must be "politics in command"—Mao's teachings —all the way; there was no room for heterodoxy and a Party split if the imperiled nation was to survive the twin threats of war with United States imperialism and/or Soviet "social imperialism." That meant self-reliance on "people's war" strategy and tactics. It meant more decentralization; spurring the masses to initiative and innovation; sending city people to learn from the peasants, and vice versa; priority for the needs of the peasants, 70 to 80 percent of the people; capital created by labor and collectively invested by the peasants themselves; and expunging all remaining bourgeois influences under mentorship of the army, "the great school of the people."

In a word, Mao demanded that the proletarian successors to power reenact the revolutionary life experience of his own generation, and reach its logical conclusions.

Thus the first issue was posed by Mao's conviction that the Party was following the revisionist (Soviet) road to capitalism—creating a new class, an elite of bureaucratic power wielders, a mandarinate of cadres divorced from labor and the people. There was a closely linked issue. That was posed by Liu's search—supported by P'eng Chen and others, according to Chairman Mao's comments to me—for a compromise in the Sino-Soviet impasse.

By 1965 the United States' bombing attacks on Vietnam, close upon China's border, threatened China with invasion. Liu wanted to send a Chinese delegation to the Soviet Twenty-third Party Congress, to reactivate the Sino-Soviet alliance. Mao resolutely refused to be drawn into a position of dependence, as in Korea, and a possible double cross. Instead, he insisted upon a posture of complete self-reliance on a people's war of defense—while continuing to build the Bomb—and heavy support for, but not intervention in, Vietnam.

Mao's line seemed madly unorthodox when viewed against the background of traditional Chinese strategy in handling threats of foreign aggression. *Yi yi chih yi*— use barbarians to fight barbarians—was an age-old cardinal principle in China, comparable to the *divide et impera* principle sacred to Rome and her successors. Among tradition-bound Chinese as well as Western Peking-ologists versed in Chinese history it was said that Mao had lost his mind. A weaker power following a policy which seemed to unite its enemies and invite a "war on two fronts"? An international propaganda offensive calling for "a plague on both their houses"? But Mao knew what he was doing. The greater threat was internal, not external. Compromising with either of the superpowers could then only lead to a split on the home front. A resolutely independent and united China could weather any storm. A China torn apart internally by factions seeking to exploit advantages of alliance with Russia could not stand.

There were many subissues and specific policies in contradiction but the above two were fundamental. Now it was said that Liu and Mao had always represented "two lines" since the beginning, when both became Communists in 1921. "Two lines" there no doubt were. In Mao's own idiom it was also a case of "nonantagonistic contradictions [gradually] becoming antagonistic" over the forty-five years during which the Party had held both of them. Personal power struggle? Subjective factors cannot be entirely separated from objective political reality, but there could be little doubt that the Mao-Liu struggle was mainly one of irreconcilable differences over means and ends affecting the fate of the great Chinese revolution itself—including, of course, the role of the personality cult.

Much has been written about the events which followed the August, 1966, decisions: the dissolution of the Party committees and para-Party organizations such as the Young Communists and the labor unions, the closing of schools (many had been closed earlier) and release of millions of non-Party youths to form Red Guard detachments and engage in overthrowing the Party elite, the free-for-all struggle for power for new leaders, and the ultimate intervention of the armed forces. In this prefatory comment it is enough to note that Mao's victory—with the help of the army—was so complete that Vice-Chairman and Defense Minister Lin Piao was able to state, at the Ninth Party Congress in 1969 (which named him Mao's constitutional successor), that "whoever opposes Chairman Mao Tse-tung's Thought, at any time or under any circumstances, will be condemned and punished by the whole Party and the whole country."

Mao's Thought had by 1970 permeated the whole nation with these aims: to speed up the erasure of differences between town and countryside; to move toward closer equalization of the material and cultural standards and opportunities of the worker, the peasant, the soldier, the cadre, and the technician-expert; to integrate shop and classroom work in everyone's education and life experience; to smash all bourgeois thought and especially its remnants among intellectuals and officials; to proletarianize higher learning by integrating students and workers and combining labor practice with classroom theory; to bring public health and medical services to the rural masses; to train everyone to bear arms and learn from the army; to create a one-class generation of many-sided, well-educated youths inspired by ideals of service to the people, at home and abroad, contemptuous of personal wealth, and dedicated to a "world outlook" anticipating the final liberation of man from hunger, greed, ignorance, war, and capitalism.

All that? Yes, and much more. I merely paraphrase words heard not just from officials and Maoist activists[8]

___

[8] An "activist" is one recognized by his group as one who not only studies and knows the Thought of Mao but "applies it in a living way."

but from all those "tempered" by Mao Thought when pinned down to define what the cultural revolution was and is all about.

Ah, but the road is long and the road is hard, and must be covered in stages. There will be more cultural revolutions to come. When eating a meal, as Mao says, one takes it mouthful by mouthful—and there must be time to savor each morsel before attacking the next.

Meanwhile, what was life like for the non-Party population—the immense majority of adults—two years after the Ninth Party Congress was told that victory had been won in the Great Proletarian Cultural Revolution?

4

Outside Citizen Wang

Citizen Wang, our man in the street, had grown neither
horns nor a halo since 1965. "Chairman Mao is always
with us," sang some small children to me in a factory
kindergarten equipped with its own air-raid shelter—a
new thing. Both they and their parents said they loved
Mao, and there seemed little reason to doubt that most
of them meant it. Yet except for the Mao badges worn by
everybody, the outward appearance of citizens still closely
resembled that of the man I had seen before the cultural
revolution.

There was more uniformity of dress: blue and gray
jackets and trousers, in the winter padded with cotton,
for both men and women, with a greater mixture of army
or militia khaki and navy pale blue. Except for their
red-starred caps and red-barred collar tabs soldiers were
indistinguishable from civilians. Many women wore
brighter and better clothes at home, where nearly all had
stored away a silk or woolen garment or two for special
occasions, but the street fashion was now proletarian.

"Wait a bit," said an old friend, "and you'll see more
variety. Just look at those women there, they're wearing a
new pattern of kerchief, with brighter colors. It means a
period of relaxation is coming." As a guest in one Chinese
household of professional people I noticed the wives

poring over lengths of gaily printed textiles spread out on a table. They were closely studying a fashion book—from Japan, think of that!

In the cities it was now harder to tell an intellectual from a peasant or a worker. Intellectuals had been brought down several more pegs and carefully cultivated their submergence in the crowd. Since nearly all children now attend school, five years had produced more literates. In urban China it is hard to find a *hsia-tzu* (blind one, as the Chinese term an illiterate) under the age of fifty. People seem more forthright and dignified in bearing, and meet one another with courtesy and a new absence of class consciousness. In new factories I found that the workers now were nearly all middle-school (high-school) graduates.

Twenty years of tree planting had beautified both the cities and the villages and a general transformation of the earth was brightening the worn face of the ancient landscape; it looked newly scrubbed. China was visibly far richer than ever before, but not in private wealth.

Citizen Wang is now well fed, healthy, adequately clad, fully employed with labor tasks, Mao classes, and technical studies, during his six-day work week. On his free day—usually a Sunday but often a week day; free days are staggered to relieve congestion—he relaxes with his family or may play ping-pong or in summer swim in a pool or river or lake or the sea—and swimming is still a sport new to China. In winter he may join hikers in the countryside. He may also volunteer to dig holes and make bricks for air-raid shelters—working alongside a physician or a teacher.

Wang belongs to a group, as everyone does. In the city he accepts discipline from his Party-line neighborhood committee, responsible for child care, sanitation and pollution control, settling disputes, welfare, health, and provision for aged and handicapped people. In the communes such tasks are shared at the village or production team level.

We cannot really see inside Citizen Wang, but if this man has worries they obviously do not include mounting food prices, medical costs, or taxes. Prices have been stable or declining for more than a decade and there is no inflation or black market. Wang pays no personal income taxes. State revenues derived from surplus labor value are hidden in the form of price controls in the state-managed market, which keeps consumption within planned necessity. Citizen Wang lives on a very narrow budget but is free from bank mortgages, debt, and the fear of starvation and beggary which plagued his parents.

His cultural life includes access to parks, playgrounds, museums, lectures, concerts, radio, television, and theater for very small fees or none at all. In 1970 his choice of books was confined to textbooks and the works of Mao. He may own a long-wave radio or may buy parts for and assemble a short-wave set. In rare instances he may have television. The Box is relatively more expensive than abroad, and television sets are usually collectively owned by one's group or institution. All programs are heavily larded with political propaganda, as is the theater. Tickets for theatrical and sports events are in great demand, and in practice (although a very few seats are sold at the box office) are available only through one's group. Movies are plentiful and cheap but offer little variety.

The wall posters our friend reads carry Mao's directives or exhortations; the newspapers, generally scanned on public bulletin boards, convey only Party-line news. Foreign news is scant and carefully screened; one reads nothing to upset the view that China, though still backward in many respects, is politically correct about everything. On the other hand, Mr. Wang is not troubled by murder stories, market plunges, pornography, race riots, divorce scandals, dope rings, muggings, commercialized sex, sadism and masochism, and class envy of the rich. There are no more rich. There are also very few corrupt officials, thieves, or other parasites. Though class enemies still exist, they are mostly responsible for evils abroad.

In short, China is, as some wit has remarked before me, a veritable sink of morality.

In everything mentioned above there is little new except more of the same, nor are wages much changed except for slight increases at the lower and middle levels and some reductions at the top. Higher army officers, for example, recently took a 30-percent voluntary cut, or so I was told by one general I met in Hangchow. Higher officials likewise. (Mao Tse-tung reportedly took a 20-percent cut in his allowance.) Above the apprentice level, factory wages ranged from $20 a month to $50—48 to 122 yuan[1]—depending on age, rank, and experience, while a few senior specialists might attain a junior general's pay of about $100. A top-ranking cadre or full general earns around $150 a month, but if he has no dependents he may return a generous portion to the state. Farmers' incomes vary widely and cash is much less than city workers' wages, but commodity income and side line benefits bring the commune dweller closer than before to equality with the urban worker.

In a dozen great cities I visited and in many county towns and commune centers I saw improved consumer necessities offered at slightly lower than 1965 prices but in improved quality. Sampling a few items, per half-kilo (1.1 pounds) in U. S. dollar equivalents: vegetables in abundance and variety in season, 1 to 2 cents; best-quality rice, 8 or 9 cents; wheat flour, 5 to 6 cents; potatoes and sweet potatoes, 2 cents; lamb, pork, and beef, 20 to 40 cents; confections and candy, 30 to 80 cents.

Formerly relatively few Chinese ever tasted fish; now it is widely sold, even in the interior, at 20 to 40 cents a half-kilo. Milk is 10 cents a quart; beer, 20 cents a bottle; sweet drinks, 5 to 10 cents; ice-cream cones and sticks, 2 to 4 cents each; grape wine (dry white and rosé), 50 cents

[1] The official exchange rate is 2.44 yuan to U. S. $1.00. For statistical purposes it is generally figured as 1 yuan = U. S. $0.40.

a bottle; gin, 55 cents; eggs, 30 cents a dozen. In a provision store run for foreigners in Peking one can buy specialty foods at slightly higher prices, including excellent black caviar at about $2.50 a pound.

Street grog shops offer a *plat du jour* of steamed wheat roll, pickled vegetables, sausage, and soup for 4 to 6 cents. A heftier meal in a factory canteen costs 10 to 15 cents. Most Chinese wear felt-soled cotton shoes, which cost $1 to $3; leather shoes are priced from $6 to $10, synthetic shoes $2 to $3. Cotton shirts are $2 to $3. Ready-made infant suits cost $2 to $4; a good fur hat, $5; lined overcoats, sheepskin or leather or cloth finished, $20 to $40; drip-dry blouse and slacks, $6 to $10.

Grain products, cooking oil, and cotton goods are still rationed. Depending upon work performed, individual grain rations vary from about 30 to 45 pounds a month; with other foods now abundant, that is more than enough. China leads the world in cotton cloth output[2] and it is a huge item in China's foreign trade and foreign exchange income. Cotton cloth inside China is therefore rationed at about 18 feet per person, including infants. Synthetics and woolens are ration free and in great demand. Cooking-oil rations are more than the average family needs. With these exceptions consumer goods are unrationed.

There are no more privately owned cars but urban and interurban bus services have improved—although the buses are still crowded. Trains in China are among the world's finest. Public transport fares are low.

Our man in the street (or village lane) probably has at least one bicycle in his family, at a cost of $35 to $45. His rent (maintenance cost) is $1 to $2 per room per month. Housing varies widely, but is generally improved. In the countryside peasants own their own homes, tax free. Industrial workers' medical expenses are met by their organizations, as likewise in the communes. Medicines cost

[2] See page 155.

a tiny fraction of prices in the West. Birth-control pills are distributed free through organizations.

Beyond that, the life style of the people can be fully seen only through further study of the cultural revolution. Its results are especially profound in organizational and political changes in factories, in lower and higher education, in the farm communes, in health services, in cultural activity of all kinds, and in the defense forces. Service in the army, navy, and air force is by far the most genuinely sought-after career among youth, and very few aspirants are chosen. A new attitude among Mao's youthful successors—in accordance with the dictum "forget self: serve the people"—is most dramatically seen in the spread of medical science and attention from the city to the countryside.

Part Two

Medical Care and Population Control

5

Abortion with Acupuncture

We are in a small hospital room to witness a new use of acupuncture. We have been conducted there by Dr. Lin Ch'iao-chih, an old friend of mine. An abortion is being performed on a smiling patient. A factory worker, aged twenty-eight, she is under no anesthesia except two needles painlessly inserted in her ear lobes.

Dr. Lin Ch'iao-chih was the first Chinese woman gynecologist graduated in England; she later did intern work in Chicago. A pioneer in modern medical practice in China, Dr. Lin has been training gynecologists and obstetricians for half a century. Still professing Christianity and belief in God—a subject on which she has occasional arguments with her friend Chou En-lai—she speaks fluent and delightful English. She apologizes for it and calls it "rusted."

"I began as a pediatrician," she says, "but I could not bear to see babies die. So I switched to bringing them into life."

Nearing sixty-nine and past retirement age, the diminutive Dr. Lin was as vivacious as ever, slight in body and strong in character. An active member of the Chinese Academy of Medical Sciences and a teacher in a medical college, she devotes four to six hours a day to her department in the former Peking Union Medical College. Once

China's most advanced hospital and medical school, the College was built with Rockefeller Foundation support more than half a century ago. During the cultural revolution it was called the Anti-Imperialist Hospital. Now it is Shou Du, Capital Hospital. About 60 percent of its doctors, nurses, and staff are women. In the obstetrics and gynecology department the percentage is 90. The medical students are about equally divided between the sexes.

The patient gives a friendly grin as she grants permission for me to photograph her during the operation. She is ten weeks pregnant. A small stainless-steel tube, attached to a Number 8 dilator, is connected to a hose which leads to a receptacle and on to compressed air and an electric pump. Negative pressure about equal to the pull of a bicycle pump is adequate for the vacuum removal: in rural areas the device can be activated by foot power. This method of abortion is now in common use down to the rural commune hospital level.

"It is simple, practically painless, there is no hemorrhage, and no severe aftereffects," Dr. Lin explains.

While the operation proceeds I learn from the patient that she has two children and does not want another. Two or three children are recommended, and the correct marriage ages in urban areas are twenty-six for women and twenty-eight for men. The later the better. "Recommended" and "correct" are still far from universal practice, but society, especially urban society, now frowns on violations. Countless marriages took place at younger ages during the cultural revolution, however, and rural folk frequently pair off at twenty to twenty-five without incurring any "punishment" or forcible separation, as has been alleged abroad.

"Do you feel any pain?" I ask in Chinese. The patient smiles and shakes her head. She uses Mao Tse-tung Thought, she says. "Fear neither hardship nor death," perhaps. In less than ten minutes she is up from the table.

Not quite convinced, I return a few days later to witness another abortion, on a young woman of twenty-nine. She works in an electrical products factory and has a six-year-old child. She has been using a uterine ring contraceptive, she says, but will now turn to the pill. Again acupuncture is the anesthesia. Just as cheerful as the first case, she seems unaware of anything happening until, surprised, she is told that it is all done. She sits up and chats a moment.

"I am now entitled to two weeks' leave with pay," she says, "but I want to go back to work this afternoon. I feel fine. The shop needs me and we all have to help fulfill our quota ahead of schedule." Dr. Lin tells her to lie down an hour or two and she can then go home.

Abortions are done free of charge and on demand of the mother alone, but preferably with family agreement. Experiments with birth control pills began in 1964. Since then the 22-day pill, developed in China, has increasingly replaced intrauterine contraceptives and other devices. It is taken from the fifth day of menstruation. All medical organizations, mobile units, and army and commune medical teams distribute control propaganda and the pills free of charge. Currently the demand exceeds production.

Obviously, abortion is not encouraged in China as a substitute for contraceptive measures. It is usually a last resort for mothers of one or more children who have not received or succeeded with contraceptive devices. Because there is no such thing as illegitimacy in China—both parents are mutually and equally responsible for the child's care—abortion is not normally a means of avoiding unmarried motherhood. A few first-pregnancy mothers do seek abortion but as a rule they are persuaded against it unless the mother's health is endangered.

Experimentation with acupuncture as anesthesis for abortion operations began in 1968 and by now is in widespread use, Dr. Lin told me. Acupuncture is also used in childbirth. (Some 90 percent of deliveries in China are by natural childbirth, but in difficult cases acupuncture or other anesthesia is used.) However, the proved success of the method—important especially in rural areas where professional anesthetists are few—had not yet been announced. To my chagrin the chairman of the Anti-Imperialist Hospital's revolutionary committee asked me not to publish the photographs of or write about what I had witnessed. Some days later I was asked about my visit by Premier Chou En-lai. He said he had for some weeks had on his desk, awaiting official approval, a news story about this use of acupuncture. Now he was satisfied, he said, and personally released a report of my hospital visit for publication. I could not imagine President Nixon or Premier Kosygin finding time for such a detail of responsibility. How could one man find the time? Chou is at least several.

6

What *Is* Acupuncture?

As a resident in prerevolutionary China I never seriously tried to understand acupuncture and moxibustion.[1] I con-·sidered empirical Chinese medicine generally quackery, as did most foreigners. On my first return visit to China, in 1960, I discovered that it merited more attention. I learned that since 1958 all Western-trained doctors had been required to devote at least six months to the study of traditional medicine, which has a written history of 2,200 years and includes thousands of volumes of writings, prescriptions, and details of diseases and their treatment.

I have had many talks with Chinese and foreign doctors about acupuncture, but the best brief summary of it I have found is still a 1961 report by Dr. William Y. Chen, a senior surgeon of the U. S. Public Health Service, which I have quoted before.[2] In the course of his general survey,

---

[1] "Moxibustion" is derived from a corruption of the Cantonese word *mongsa*, for Chinese wormwood (*Artemesia moxa*). The leaves of moxa are prepared in a soft woolly mass and used as a cautery for burning on the skin, as part of an ancient empirical science similar to the cauterization healing said to be still practiced in parts of Europe.

[2] In *Red China Today, op. cit.*, pages 299–300, 305–06, 308. Some of the material in this section is from that book and its original edition, titled *The Other Side of the River: Red China Today* (New York, 1962).

based on his personal knowledge of China, an examination of data from foreign doctors recently there, and an analysis of research in specialized medical journals of China (twenty-five of "major importance"), Dr. Chen offered this comment about acupuncture:

> Traditional Chinese medicine is an empirical healing art based on 4,000 years of practical experience. Its simple concept of health and disease is the functional bodily harmony or disharmony between two forces, *Yin* (the negative) and *Yang* (the positive). Anatomically and physiologically traditional Chinese medicine has practically nothing to offer; yet the vast volumes on herbs and drugs and medical treatises recording observations of diseases are precious. The results of the use of these drugs and healing arts of acupuncture, moxibustion, massage, and breathing therapy certainly have their empirical value. . . .
>
> Acupuncture . . . consists of the introduction of hot and cold needles into the body at specific points. The needles may be either fine or coarse, short or long (from 3 cm. to 24 cm.). . . . When the needles puncture and stimulate different tissues or organs at various depths, they cause physiological reactions and thus produce healing results.

Acupuncturists were now required to learn aseptic techniques and basic anatomy and science in courses comparable to those given "secondary doctors." They were all attached to hospitals, nearly all of which had acupuncture specialists. Many of them used low-voltage electrically charged needles. Treatment was sometimes combined with radiotherapy. Dr. Chen went on:

> The hypothesis is that stimulation from punctures is conducted from the peripheral nerves to the brain cortex and suppresses pathological irritation in the brain. Such an explanation seems to be in harmony with the Pavlovian theory of conditioned reflex.
>
> Acupuncture has been widely used in practically all kinds of diseases ranging from surgical conditions such

as appendicitis to chronic conditions such as diabetes. It is believed that it produces best results in illness of the nervous system or those of neurological origin. Good results have been reported in the treatment of facial paralysis, arthritis, and eczema. One Russian physician reported that his long history of miserable arthritis was much improved by acupuncture. A doctor from India who went to China and studied acupuncture in 1958 entertained certain doubts as to its value at first. However, he believed afterwards that the integration of traditional medicine and Western medicine had already accomplished remarkable success. He was also treated successfully by acupuncture for his acute sinusitis.[3]

I myself have met patients in hospitals in Peking and other cities being treated by traditional Chinese means for appendicitis, eczema, rheumatism, sinusitis, tuberculosis, migraine headaches, bronchitis, and various kinds of neurasthenia. In Hankow I met a patient who had arrived at the hospital unconscious with what Western-trained surgeons had diagnosed as acute appendicitis. Treated by empirical medicine and acupuncture, he was being dismissed as cured.

Chinese herbal medicine and acupuncture work together and herbalists are often needle men as well. Translations of traditional Chinese medical terminology are difficult, but the *yin-yang* concept of "contradictions" is basic. The body is an organic unity; illness is caused by imbalances between different organs or their extensions, and cure consists in restoring balance and harmony. This is done by relaxing "antagonisms" among eight principal lines of tension: *yin-yang* (negative-positive), *piuo-li* (outer-inner), *leng-je* (hot-cold), and *hsu-shih* (empty-solid).

In the compleat guide to acupuncture the body is charted in terms of those principles and of "life forces" of balance between them. Normally "contradictions" of a

[3] From "Medicine and Public Health," *China Quarterly*, No. 6, April-June, 1961.

nonantagonistic nature exist in an equilibrium. When "disunity" (disease) occurs, one organ or set of functions has been overworked, overstimulated, injured, or otherwise disturbed. The doctor's task is to restore the balance by removing the cause of the antagonism or congestion.

"Diseases have inner and outer causes," I was told during an earlier visit to the Anti-Imperialist Hospital (when it was called the Peking Union Hospital). The speaker was the vice-director, Dr. Hsu Hung-t'u. He said: "The higher nervous system of the brain affects the general physiology, of course. What we call *ni-ch'u chung-kuan* [anger-in-a-state-of-fury-burns[4]] may cause organic pains and injuries elsewhere. A patient may arrive complaining of pains which a Western diagnosis may show to be due to hypertension but a Chinese doctor may treat by a combination of medicine and acupuncture.

"A Western-style doctor often only asks the medical symptoms and medical history. A Chinese doctor looks upon the person as a unity subject to both outside and inside tensions. He wants to know about the person's family, his relations with his parents, whether he likes his wife, how his work goes, what his personal resentments are, where disharmony exists in his life, whether he is a native of the city or is a southerner or a northerner. All these go into diagnosis."

"South or north? That makes a difference?"

"Yes, certain medicines 'hot' for a northerner give the southerner a 'cold' reaction."

"Such an inquiry would also have to touch upon the patient's political thought, I presume?"

"Of course—conflicts of all kinds are discussed."

From this and subsequent conversations it seems clear that the traditional Chinese pathologist was something of an analyst and psychiatrist as well and that acupuncture was often used as shock therapy. Whether illnesses caused

---

[4] The general idea, not an exact translation!

by unresolved stress or anxiety are greater in modern China than in the frenetic competitive system of the United States I do not know. Dr. Chen, whom I have already quoted, reported that the incidence of hypertensive heart disease—for whatever this proves—was about the same in both countries.[5] I have no statistics on neurasthenic diseases in China but the number of cases I have encountered in hospitals and sanatoria seems very high. The inner tensions caused by social pressures of the kind of system Communists are trying to create are obviously severe, outlets are few, and it is not surprising that the demand for consultations with Chinese therapists is great.

"Whether the Communists will succeed in their ambitious endeavor to produce a new Chinese medical science by incorporating traditional medicine with modern scientific medicine only time can tell," concluded Dr. Chen. "Whatever the outcome, its development is worthy of our constant attention."[6]

The late Aldous Huxley, the British novelist who was an ardent believer in acupuncture, reported as early as 1957 that "International Congresses of Acupuncture are now convened," and that several hundred European doctors were trying to "combine the science and art of Western medicine with the ancient science and art of Chinese acupuncture." He continued:

> That a needle stuck into the outside surface of the leg a little below the knee [elsewhere, needles may penetrate much deeper; expertly handled, they draw no blood] should affect the functioning of the liver is obviously incredible. . . . In the normally healthy organism [the Chinese maintain] there is a continuous circulation of energy. . . . Acupuncture redirects and normalises the flow of energy.

[5] Medical sources in China say it is definitely less there now.
[6] William Y. Chen, *op. cit.*

According to Chinese acupuncturists, the limbs, trunk, and head are lined with invisible "meridians" related in some way to the various organs of the body. Huxley accepts that "as a matter of empirical fact." He goes on to say:

> On these meridians are located specially sensitive points. A needle inserted at one of these points will affect the functioning of the organ related to the meridian on which the point lies. By pricking at a number of judiciously selected points the skilled acupuncturist re-establishes the normal circulation of energy and brings the patient back to health.
>
> Once again we are tempted to shrug our shoulders and say that it makes no sense. But then, reading the proceedings of the most recent Congress of Acupuncture, we learn that experimenters have been able, by means of delicate electrical measuring instruments, to trace the course of the Chinese meridians, and that when a strategic point is pricked with a needle relatively large changes of electrical state can be recorded.[7]

Huxley related that among the pathological symptoms "on which the old Chinese methods work very well" are "various kinds of undesirable mental states—certain kinds of depression and anxiety, for example—which, being presumably related to organic derangements, disappear as soon as the normal circulation of energy is restored. Results which several years on the analyst's couch have failed to produce may be obtained, in some cases, by two or three pricks with a silver needle."

Enthusiasm for the therapeutic benefits of both acupuncture and herbalism may be kept within bounds when it is remembered that strictly Chinese medical literature offered scarcely any knowledge of such basic sciences as bacteriology, microbiology, parasitology, epidemiology,

[7] The *Observer*, London, October 22, 1961.

endocrinology, venereology, etc., and only primitive concepts of asepsis. Chinese medical doctrine was virtually useless in the prevention of smallpox, typhus, tuberculosis, plague, dysentery, cholera, tetanus, kala azar, malaria, filariasis, syphilis, and some other diseases. Even in 1971 it is perhaps still too early for a layman to say whether those in China who presumably continue to oppose the policy of integration of native and Western therapies may not be proved justified in some of their doubts.

Up to the mid-1960s it seemed to me that some doctors I encountered in hospitals were embarrassed by the prestige being given to traditional methods. Many must have at least resented the *compulsion* to study them—something like requiring all Western doctors to learn osteopathy. In its impact on Western-educated medical men, the cultural revolution, with its intensified emphasis on reaching deep into rural China with their services, was accompanied by a humbler attitude toward the view of the masses about what works and doesn't work. The effectiveness of acupuncture, and new techniques developed in its application, had by the 1970s rendered it both more popular and more impressive in results claimed for it.[8]

"There is as yet no general anatomical theory to explain acupuncture," said Dr. Lin Chiao-chih, as we discussed new applications of the method of anesthesis in the removal of huge abdominal tumors, in chest surgery, and even in open-heart operations. "Thousands of our scientists are working on the problem and we expect an early 'breakthrough,' " she concluded.

[8] American doctors visiting China in 1971 have brought back new and interesting material on current uses of acupuncture. See, for example, Dr. E. Grey Dimond's "Acupuncture Anesthesia," *Journal of the American Medical Association*, Vol. 218, No. 10, December 6, 1971.

7

Sex and Demography

That glimpse into one ward of one hospital reflects one major change in health services: increased spread and utilization of all practical means of birth control. But Dr. Lin and her staff spend far more time bringing babies into the world than keeping them out, in such tasks as halting uterine cancer and treatment to make childbearing possible, and in participating in the nation-wide program to "put the stress on rural areas first" popularized by the cultural revolution.

Broadly speaking, four principles are now observed— Mao Tse-tung's guidelines laid down for medical and health workers: 1) put prevention first; 2) serve the needs of workers, peasants, and soldiers; 3) combine rural and urban public health measures with mass movements; and 4) unite Chinese traditional and Western-trained doctors.

"Prevention first" means far more than family planning, but that is now so basic that it requires further discussion before reporting other applications of the term.

How effective was the Chinese pill? According to Dr. Lin and other specialists, their 22-day pill was entirely free of side effects. It was 100 percent effective if taken daily, but oversights (intentional or otherwise) were "still far too many." Meanwhile, a most intensive search went on for an ideal once-a-month pill. Experiments had been conducted all over China since 1969, said Dr. Lin. In Peking alone 5,000 people were involved in a control project which included medical personnel and workers and their families.

China is also in touch with world studies and results, especially in Japan, of the menses-inducing vaginal pill which utilizes prostaglandins. "And," said Dr. Lin, "our experimental group—we call it the Family Planning Fighters Group—is also working on longer-term oral contraceptives. We are experimenting with once-in-three-months pills and we now believe we can develop a pill or vaccine effective for about a year." Tests are also continuing with Chinese herbal remedies as contraceptives for both men and women (but no one has yet found a way to use acupuncture for this purpose!). Male sterilization (after two children) is advocated, is free, and is not popular.

How extensive is availability and application of contraceptives? In the provinces I visited the pill was reported everywhere in use, even far back in Shensi, but Dr. Lin said the supply had not yet caught up with demand. There are roughly seventy to eighty million women of childbearing age, which would imply the need for an output of about seventeen billion 22-day pills annually. Contraceptives for males help make up the present gap.

China also needs billions of vaccines for various contagious and epidemic diseases and is already quite the largest producer in that field. One "ultramodern" laboratory visited in Peking—and described to me by a visiting Dutch doctor, J. A. DeHaas, as larger than any single plant in Europe—had an output of eighty million vaccine units a year. My old friend, American-born Dr. George Hatem,[1] told me he had seen more than a dozen labs with about the same capacity in other areas of China.

---

[1] For an account of his extraordinary career—he has been called "the man who wiped out venereal disease in China"—see *Red China Today, op. cit.*, pages 261–77.

I was officially informed that about 70 percent of women of childbearing age in Peking use contraceptives and that two-thirds of them take the pill. In rural communes covering ten counties which surround Peking about 40 percent of the women of relevant age were now depending on the pill.

No national statistics on population increase had been published for more than a decade, and figures given me in different localities varied widely. In greater Peking the rate was officially put at 1.6 percent for 1969, for example; in a commune near Shanghai I was told it was just 1 percent; in greater Sian an official estimated it at 3 percent.

The rate of growth is at any rate still too high to please Chairman Mao. Speaking to him about progress in general I said I was pleased to find contraceptives used far more widely these days. "Now at least no one objects to birth control."

I had been taken in, he said. In the countryside if a woman's first child is a girl she wants to have a boy. If the second is a girl, again she wants a boy. The third one comes, a girl again, and she still tries for a boy. Soon there are nine of them, all are girls, by then she is already forty-five, so she can only leave it at that!

"Yes, but now there aren't many people opposed—I mean, young people don't object to birth control . . . ?"

Mao said that they still attach importance to males and look down on women. He thought it was perhaps also true in the United States. This must be changed—but it takes time to change fixed ideas.

Mao's skepticism about birth control in "without sons" families, as well as doubts he expressed concerning census reports, made me recall my first encounter, in 1965, with Ch'en Yung-kuei, the much-publicized leader of the celebrated Ta Chai brigade, of a commune in mountainous Shansi. Ch'en had led his 360 people—178 able-bodied adults—in the laborious building of new fertile land torn from the clay and rock cliffs by hand tools. They brought in irrigation, buttressed by miles of stone walls, they planted orchards, they fought a lone self-reliant battle with stubborn nature, and they won. Within a decade they increased grain output to three tons an acre, a record for that forbidding land. Ch'en was a natural leader, vigorous, intelligent, and all peasant. I asked him about "family planning" in his commune. The term seemed unfamiliar to him. I said I meant "birth control."

"Oh, that." He grinned. "No, we don't need that. We need able-bodied workers."

I asked farmer Ch'en how many births were registered in his brigade in 1964. "Eight," he answered at once. And how many deaths? "We didn't lose anybody," he said. Not even a great-grandfather? He scratched his head. He remembered that one old landlord had expired. "If you call that a death," he added. "He hadn't been able-bodied for years!"

It was common enough to meet peasant men and women in their late thirties or forties who (now somewhat shamefacedly) admitted to five or six or more children, the older ones usually girls. The old fatalistic view that in order for one child to survive it is necessary to produce half a dozen or more is also hard to shake off. (And I have met plenty of older people whose experience was just that.) Peasant mothers-in-law and grandparents out of old habit go on pushing their young ones to overproduce.

In 1964 Premier Chou had told me that his government hoped to see population growth drop below 2 percent by 1970. Now when I asked him about that he said that by 1966 the national rate actually did fall below 2 percent. It shot up again during the cultural revolution, he added, when millions of Red Guards went on "long marches" and the sexes freely intermingled. Many early marriages helped boost the birth rate. That period of aberration passed, with dispersion of the Red Guards—back to school or to regular work—and restoration of discipline. With wider use of the convenient new pill, the Premier thought the rate was again on the decline.

Foreigners are naturally curious (and so are Chinese!) about the effect the pill may have, particularly among the young, on the prevalent strict attitudes toward sexual relations. In pre-Communist China an unmarried woman could lose her marriageability (or might be stoned or mobbed) if seen, however innocently, wandering down a country lane alone with a man. At the same time impoverished families sold girl children into concubinage, prostitution, or slavery. All that has vanished, former "outlets" for the bachelor or discontented married male seeking dalliance are closed, seduction is a serious matter, and rape a grave crime.

Coeducation is universal and unmarried young men and women work together at many things, but not in bed. One or two instances of pairing off for a bicycle ride are enough to establish the couple as engaged. Breaking off such an arrangement brings social disgrace, especially for the male. Even going to eat lunch under a tree with a boy when sharing work in a commune can compromise a girl. That is what I learned from a few hours' talk, in the home of friends, with a teenage ex–Red Guard.

Does a tacitly "engaged" couple ever make love? "Instances of premarital relations are really rare," replied a doctor friend. "As for actual promiscuity, it is regarded as a deviation requiring social discipline or, in repeated cases, reform in confinement. Extramarital intercourse is uncommon but it occurs more often than premarital intercourse."

Chinese are easily upset by questions of this kind, but I had established bona fides for my inquiry when, in 1965, I asked a vice-director of the Women's and Children's Health Administration of Peking about premarital abstinence—in a country where ideal marriage ages were deferred to twenty-six for women and twenty-eight for men.

(In rural China the recommended marriage ages are twenty-three for women, twenty-five for men.) Foreigners found it very hard to believe, I said, that chastity could be universal in such circumstances.

She pointed out that women now have productive work to do and the same opportunities as men; that in the past it was a disgrace if a girl was not married before twenty whereas now the view was the opposite; and that young people were disciplined by political belief and ideals of work for society. They did not live for pleasure alone.

"All that is true—and there is also the absence of commercialized sex stimulation in a hundred ways seen in the West. Still, shouldn't a free woman have the freedom at least to get acquainted with the man she may choose to marry?"

"Well, it is not that strict. There is a time when a man and woman reach an understanding and start getting acquainted. We don't deny that premarital sex sometimes exists, and that pregnancy sometimes occurs, though it is rare. In the past such women self-aborted, or tried to, but now, owing to use of contraceptives and the knowledge that free abortion is available, that seldom happens.

"There are very few cases of abortion by unmarried mothers. Considering the immensity of our population the number is so small it cannot be a serious problem. Whenever abortion is sought for a first child the doctor tries to persuade the woman to retain it. If, in the case of an unmarried mother, marriage offers no way out—because the father is already married, or because it is a bad match politically or otherwise—no one will insist upon the birth. The abortion is performed."

The foregoing observations were generally confirmed in conversations I had with Dr. George Hatem, who has a son and a daughter by his beautiful Chinese wife. In the case of his son, who "went steady" for six years, he and his girl had no "carnal relations" in their entire premarital courtship. That's what George thinks. Anyway, they recently married, at the correct ages, and then quickly produced a grandson for the Hatems.

"That's the way it is with young people I know," said Dr. Hatem, who sees scores of patients daily. "I won't say that the pill may not change matters. Everything changes here. But right now our young people are probably the least permissively sex-oriented in the world."

In any event, whether sex begins to swing more freely or not, the free pill and free abortion are likely soon—after many years of family planning propaganda to break down peasant conservatism and male chauvinism—to bring about an increased fall in the rate of population growth. But China is an egalitarian society of immense numbers, where benefits of progress must be shared by all, and a corresponding rise in the standard of living must cover a vast area of humanity.

So how many Chinese are there now? This question for many years sent foreign demographers far astray in their speculations. Their main problem was that they continued to regard as sacrosanct figures published by Peking in 1954 on the basis of what was called China's "first modern census." The total then given was 583 million; in 1957 a "sampling census" reported 646 million. In 1960 all Chinese officials I met used the figure 650 million. There was one exception: Politburo member and Shanghai mayor K'o Ching-shih referred to "China's 685 million."

Five years later I asked Chairman Mao if he could give me the results of a "sampling census" reportedly taken the year before. He replied that he really did not know—some said that there were 680 to 690 million but he did not believe it. How could there be so many!

"Isn't it possible to reach a close estimate based on cloth-ration coupons alone?" I asked.

Mao replied that the peasants sometimes confused the picture. Before Liberation they had hidden births of sons, in particular, to keep them off the register and avoid conscription by Chiang Kai-shek. Since Liberation there had been a tendency to report greater numbers and less land, and to minimize harvests while exaggerating the effects of calamities. Nowadays a new birth was reported at once but if someone died then it might not be worth mentioning for months. No doubt there had been a real decline in the birth rate, but the decline in the death rate was probably greater. Average longevity had gone up from about thirty years, he concluded, to close to fifty years.

Chairman Mao's answer implied that some village communes might be finding it convenient not to register deaths in order to continue using the deceased's cotton-cloth ration and to minimize harvests in order to retain more for consumption at home. His skepticism about past and current demographic research was very disconcerting to some of the Western demographers, who had already reached figures of more than 800 million people in China.

If one took the Chairman's minimum of 680 million, and a minimum (probably underestimated, according to Premier Chou's remark to me) of 2 percent annual growth for the six years since January, 1965, then an estimate for today would bring the figure to about 780 million. In January, 1971, I asked the Premier whether one could now say that China's population had reached 800 million. He hesitated and replied, "No, not quite yet."

Until Peking wishes to be more explicit, it seems safe to assume that the population by 1972 will, with Taiwan (about 14 million), pass the 800 million mark. Even a 1 percent growth rate from now on would mean more than a billion by 2000 A.D. Two percent theoretically could add an extra 250 million by the same date.

The margin of grain supplies in excess of population growth was now a comfortable one. In January, 1971, Premier Chou provided me with harvest results in 1970— a total of 240 million tons of grain, with an additional 40 million tons in national reserves. That output was an increase of 70 to 80 percent over the "hardship years" of

1959-62. Chinese planners would be happy to get the growth rate down to 1 percent or less, however. That is their goal over the next decade of sustained effort toward a rapid advance in the rate of national savings and increased industrial production.

8

Some Special Situations

No doubt it was not just Red Guards and romancing that caused an upturn in the population growth rate during the cultural revolution, but also a severe shake-up in the entire medical profession and a disruption in existing control services. Universities were closed for nearly three years, middle schools for two years, premedical and medical studies were interrupted, personnel were dispersed, Party leadership of hospital management systems was upset or dissolved, and the new public health organizations were slow in formation, under army direction, in 1968.

One must be wary of being "taken in" by any official presentation which ignored—as most did—the price paid in lost professional hours in public health work during the revolutionary change of pace. It would be ingenuous not to ask how much of the greater reliance on acupuncture and traditional therapy was necessitated by the absence of countless medical workers sent to "learn from the peasants" while doing a period at labor tasks for which others were better suited. No satisfactory answers were offered to such questions, and it was not possible yet for an outsider to conclude whether the benefits of the new approach fully outweighed some reverses.

Work in the advanced sciences was not greatly disturbed by the cultural revolution, apparently, and some notable progress was made in several directions other than nuclear developments. In September, 1965, Chinese biochemists had succeeded in making biologically active protein in the form of synthetic insulin, becoming the first in the world to achieve this. Progress in the treatment of mutilated limbs continued and by the 1970s China seemed ahead of the world in that field. Techniques of reimplantation of severed fingers, toes, hands, feet, arms, and legs were now so widely taught that operations of the kind were frequently performed in relatively primitive rural hospitals.

It was in a large municipal hospital of Shanghai that I had, in 1964, shaken a hand which had been severed for more than two hours before it was picked up from the shop floor and then reattached to the wrist of its owner, a worker who lost it in an industrial accident. He was using it again in a near-normal function. Now I met, in 1970, in a small commune hospital in Kwangtung province, a patient who had almost recovered the use of his hand after an operation which reimplanted four severed fingers.

Another technique in which the Chinese have achieved results said to be unequaled in the West is the treatment of serious burns. Many instances are cited of recovery by people suffering third-degree burns with damage to as much as 60 percent of the body. I saw one such case myself, and many details of this rather gruesome subject are impressively documented in the report of the English traumatologist Dr. Joshua Horn,[1] who taught and practiced in China for more than a decade prior to his departure in 1969.

The question naturally arises whether the accident rate is abnormally high in Chinese industry. Statistics given to me at factories in various localities did not seem excessive, but national records had not been published on this item, as for so many others, since 1960. During the brief

[1] *Away with All Pests!* (London, 1969; New York, 1970).

"Hundred Flowers" period of free criticism (1957) many accusations of inadequate precautions were made.[2] Safety conditions had improved, with further modernization, in several factories I revisited. One benefit of combining shop work with classroom study, from higher primary school on, was to teach everybody respect and care for machines as well as how to use them.

While with Dr. Lin in Peking we visited a whole ward of women convalescing from cancer of a special type: choriocarcinoma, a cancer in the uterus. This dreadful wild cell attacks the trophoblasts and quickly rises to cause metastasis of the liver. "Formerly it was thought to be inoperable," said Dr. Lin. "People used to say, 'If you say you have cured choriocarcinoma then your patient did not *have* choriocarcinoma.' Now we use a combined treatment including chemotherapy. We save about 61 percent of the cases even when cancer has metastasized and spread to the chest. In about 40 percent of them the uterus is saved."

Dr. Lin paused to introduce us to one of her fellow surgeons, Tai Yu-hua, who had herself been cured of choriocarcinoma by chemotherapy. Her uterus had been saved and she had since delivered a healthy baby. Tears came to Dr. Tai's eyes as Dr. Lin explained that her recovery had been partly due to faith healing—faith in Mao Tse-tung. Dr. Tai's baby was called "Strong Constitution." Meaning good health? Not at all. The child was so named in honor of the new constitution adopted by the Ninth Party Congress! (In Shensi, later on, I was naturally less surprised when I met a peasant woman whose two small children were named "Antirevisionist" and "Antiimperialist." Don't ask me to explain: that's China—and cultural revolution.)

Dr. Lin had volunteered to do rural medical work and had only recently returned from half a year in a commune

[2] Roderick MacFarquhar, *The Hundred Flowers* (London, New York, 1960).

in Hunan, south of the Yangtze River. There she helped to train midwives and "barefoot doctors," so called because they work in the fields right along with other peasants. A large percentage of urban medical personnel has gone into the interior to practice in farm communes and to teach these young "barefoot doctors" to perform services at about the level of trained nurses. Their training—some are sent to county or city hospitals—is paid for by their teams or brigades and they remain commune members.

Dr. Lin continued: "Peasants like barefoot doctors, on the spot, rather than dependence on hospitals. Of course we need both, but for minor illnesses and accidents barefoot doctors are the answer. They are also prime carriers of pills and education in family planning."

9

"Stressing the Rural Areas First"

Change of scene. We are now in another general hospital in Peking. It has some 800 beds, 13 departments, 251 Western-trained doctors, 9 traditional doctors, 254 nurses, and 11 wards. It handles 2,500 to 3,000 outpatients daily. It was built and was originally staffed by Soviet Russians, when it was known as the Sino-Soviet Friendship Hospital. During the cultural revolution it was renamed Fan-hsiu I-yuan, or Antirevisionist Hospital and is now called Yo-Yi, Friendship Hospital.

We are to take a tour of the wards, but first we sit at a long table with Wang Kuang-chou, a representative of the revolutionary committee of the Public Health Bureau of Peking; two "responsible persons" (meaning committee heads) of the People's Liberation Army propaganda team of the hospital; Chang Wei-shen, a well-known pediatrician and another old friend of mine, formerly deputy director of the hospital and now a manual worker at a "poor and middle peasants" brigade in a distant commune (here on a brief leave of absence); and ten other medical workers and revolutionary committee members, including five women.

Before hearing from this committee on changes wrought by the cultural revolution, it is useful to be reminded of the staggering dimensions of the health problems inherited by the People's Republic twenty years ago. Again I shall rely on the documented report presented to a symposium of American doctors by Dr. William Y. Chen, of the U.S. Public Health Service.

"Before the Communist regime took control . . ." he wrote, "medical and public health organizations were still in their infancy and far below modern standards. Poverty and disease were the rule." Four million people a year died from "infectious and parasitic diseases" and sixty million people required "facilities for daily treatment." The scope of the problem was indicated by Dr. Chen's estimate of China's needs at what he considered "a minimum standard" of one doctor for 1,500 people and five hospital beds for 1,000 persons.

"The total number of scientifically trained doctors [in 1949] was estimated to be only 12,000; for about 500 hospitals, the country was only capable of producing 500 medical graduates per year . . ." and it had a total of 71,000 hospital beds.

"Because 84 percent of the total population in the rural areas was incapable of paying for private medical care, the only early solution of such a tragedy was believed to be a system of state (or socialized) medicine." That opinion was held by leading Chinese doctors as early as 1937, and "the idea of the county health centre system was planned, shaped and conducted mostly by American-trained doctors; many of them are now still living in China and, in fact, form the backbone of China's medical and health structure."

Hospital beds and doctors qualified in Western terms increased four to five times in the first ten years. This was far below Dr. Chen's "minimum standard," but he reported "greater strides in the improvement of sanitation, health education, and prevention [work] . . . Typhus, relapsing fever and other 'notifiable' or 'reportable' infectious diseases have been brought under control. Great improvements have been made also in the control of major parasitic diseases . . . Millions of malaria patients have been treated and its incidence rate has apparently dropped to less than a 3 percent level . . ." and 36,000,000 patients were cured of hookworm.[1]

A report that startled Old China Hands, brought back by British doctors who visited the People's Republic only seven years after the revolution, concerned "the successful control of flies, the litterless streets and fanatical household cleanliness." Professor Brian Maegraith, dean of the Liverpool School of Tropical Medicine, described mass work of village health committees and street sanitation and hygiene as "having a profound effect on the spread of gastro-intestinal infections." A single paragraph was particularly arresting to anyone who knew the squalor of rural China in the past:

One further method of control [of schistosome snails, carriers of schistosomiasis], which goes on all the time, illustrates the degree of general cooperation obtained. Until artificial fertilizers can be developed on a big enough scale, human excreta remains the cheapest and most valuable manure. Fortunately the dangerous schistosome eggs do not live long if left in faeces without contact with water. Storage thus renders the material non-infective. Thanks to skillful propaganda, this essential conservation of night soil is becoming an economic and social fact. Each family now has its own privy, a portable gaily colored pot. Every morning the contents are poured into large communal earthenware containers, which are sealed when full and left for the appropriate time necessary for the ammonia generated to kill the eggs, after which the faeces are safe for use in the fields. The collection of family night soil is assured by paying the family for it pro rata, so many cents a day per person, according to age. This scheme is also being used for the control of water pollu-

[1] Dr. William Y. Chen, *op. cit.*

tion by fishermen, for each boat now has its own collecting pot, which is regarded as a source of income.[2]

Old China Hands were not alone in their astonishment. In 1960, when I asked the good Christian Dr. Lin what was for her the most unexpected result of the revolution she exclaimed: "The flies! I never thought they could get rid of the flies!"

By 1970 all epidemic and contagious diseases had been exterminated or brought under control and reduced, including schistosomiasis and leprosy. Venereal disease had (believe it or not) disappeared in the twenty-six provinces (and even in Tibet was under control)—so much so that the venereology section of the Institute of Skin Diseases in Peking was dissolved and Dr. Hatem was able to go into well-deserved semiretirement as a clinician. Polio, measles, typhoid, and typhus were prevented by vaccines and hygienic measures. In 1969 only two cases of dysentery had appeared among about 900,000 patients seen at the Antirevisionist Hospital. Currently the two major causes of death were cardiovascular diseases and cancer.

Now, to return to Dr. Wang Kuang-chou, from the Bureau of Public Health. His responsibility covers the Special Administrative Area of Peking, with a population of about six million, including ten suburban counties with 280 people's communes. In it there are seventeen municipal hospitals and thirty district hospitals with a total of 29,000 beds, not including beds in communes and factory clinics. The area has 8,600 medical college graduates—an increase of 59 percent since 1960, plus about 2,000 traditional-medicine doctors.[3]

[2] *New Scientist*, London, December 31, 1957.

[3] No official figures were available on a national scale, but the best estimate given was about 150,000 medical college (six-year-course) graduates and some 400,000 "middle doctors" with two to four years of medical training.

Wang Kuang-chou offers us some facts concerning recent "revolutionary changes":

"In 1965 Chairman Mao said: 'The Ministry of Health is an urban overlord. In medical and health work put the stress on the rural areas.' [One becomes inured to repetition—like politics—in command.] We now study and apply Chairman Mao in a living way. In the past three years 3,600 of our medical and health workers of Peking have gone to the countryside. We have organized 6,000 medical and health workers in 430 mobile health teams, going as far as Szechuan, Yunnan, and Inner Mongolia. Our doctors, nurses, and cadres share this work in rotation.

"Barefoot doctors in the area number 13,000. They are of both sexes and their average age is twenty. They receive three months' training in medical or hospital schools—combining Western medicine and acupuncture—and then return to work for a time in communes under local hospital supervision. They then come back for another three months of training. Minor ailments are treated by them in the patient's home or at a brigade hospital; they take more serious cases to the commune hospitals. Only difficult cases now come to the city hospitals."

Besides training barefoot doctors, all hospitals train Red Medical Workers, attached to neighborhood or factory clinics, and People's Liberation Army Medical Workers. Peking had 2,164 army medical workers "serving the people" at 335 first-aid stations in the city. The Anti-revisionist Hospital was currently training forty-one such youths, for periods of three months. It had also sent eight of its staff to join a team of fifty people doing medical work in Guinea.

"Last year ninety-six medical workers from this hospital went to the countryside to settle down and stay. About one-third of our staff is always out on rotational work in the field. The mobile medical teams have these tasks: to serve the masses in a direct way, providing preventive and therapeutic services and 'putting prevention first'; to train local basic medical personnel; to promote planned parenthood; to raise the level of existing services and public health work; to combine Western and traditional medicine; to promote revolutionary socialist thinking among medical workers by living in the same houses as the workers, peasants, and soldiers, eating the same food, working their way, studying with them, and criticizing bourgeois ways."

Communes are collectives and from their own welfare funds—to which workers contribute—they provide health insurance for members. In the city, hospitals make health insurance contracts with factories and other organizations, which draw from their welfare funds, also helped by state contributions. Workers pay for their food (20 to 30 cents a day) but hospitalization is free.

I turn to Chang Wei-shen, visiting down from the countryside, lean, bronzed, and graying at the temples. I have known him since I lectured at Yenching (Peking) University more than thirty years ago, when he was a medical student there. He studied medicine in the United States and then returned to work for China. It is years since we met. He still speaks excellent English.

"Lao Chang," I say, "what took you away from Peking?"

"I am one of the ninety-six medical workers from our hospital who went to the communes to stay. Now I work in a production brigade of the Tsa Yui People's Commune, in Ta Hsing county. We have 800 people in the brigade."

"Who sent you there?"

"No one sent me. I asked to go, to integrate with the peasants and to remold my ideology. Before that I was director of the pediatrics department here and deputy director of the hospital. I did not realize I was a reactionary until the cultural revolution. When I worked with mobile medical teams I realized for the first time how much in need of medicine and doctors the peasants are. I went down as a cadre, to do manual labor, but the peasants learned that I was a doctor and they came to me for help.

"At first they called me 'hsien-sheng,' or 'elder born,' treating me like an intellectual. They said 'beg' when they asked for treatment. I labored days and nights with them at planting and harvest time. Now they call me 'Lao Chang' [Old Chang] and we are equals. I am very happy with them and determined to spend my life there. I was divorced from politics and the masses in the past. I also did not know acupuncture and traditional medicine. Now I have studied it and found it is very effective for many things. So I have learned a lot. I no longer miss city life. I am training young medical workers where they are needed. There are broad vistas in the countryside."

And his family? They are still in Peking. He comes back to visit them once a month. Perhaps he will be called back to the city again when the new Party needs him— and when he has trained young people to carry on his work at the brigade. Or his family may move to the country, to join him.

This selection from many hours of talk with doctors, barefoot doctors, nurses, patients, and medical revolutionary committeemen may at least convey some sense or atmosphere of public health work in China, in an era when attention has been turned from the privileged city and its self-centered professionalism to the fields and villages of the interior. Some 70 to 80 percent of the people live there—people who brought the Chinese Communists to power.

"The peasants are all wholehearted and enthusiastic supporters of Chairman Mao," said Lao Chang. In the eleven communes we visited I heard nothing to contradict that, but it should not be concluded that they have all become models of socialist man. Mao has no illusions that the peasant soul itself is yet free from a "spontaneous desire to become a capitalist," as he puts it. Something about that, and other commune problems, belongs to a later section.

Part Three

The Great Proletarian Cultural Revolution

IO

Cooling the Cult

Before looking more closely at the society emerging from the recent internal struggle, one must penetrate a bit deeper into the origins and the nature of the GPCR (Great Proletarian Cultural Revolution). What was complex enough at the outset was then complicated and confused by the propagandive distortions of a hot war of which the public heard mainly the accusations of the victors.

It is difficult enough to disentangle even the currently visible threads of this fascinating history, and we may not for many years see *all* the threads or be able to reveal a brief, clear pattern of what happened. Whole books have already appeared about the GPCR, and I personally know of five more "definitive" volumes now in preparation by Western scholars. But no book about China today can avoid grappling with the subject because it is still in a process of "becoming." Beneath the unity seemingly restored at the Ninth Party Congress in 1969, there continues a dialectic which may again erupt in open "struggle between two lines," as the Party idiom has it, for control of the helm of the revolution.

"All the members of the Party and all the people of our country must not think that after one, two, three, or four great cultural revolutions there will be peace and quiet.

They must always be on the alert and never relax their vigilance,"[1] said Mao Tse-tung in 1967. Even after "classes are eliminated," he declared elsewhere, "ideological and political struggles . . . will continue to occur; they will never cease . . . *Disequilibrium is a general, objective rule . . . Disequilibrium is normal and absolute whereas equilibrium is temporary and relative."*[2]

One key to comprehending events of 1966 to date is the central role played by the cult of personality of Mao Tse-tung, a factor he himself has freely acknowledged. In one sense the whole struggle was over control of the cult and by whom and above all "for whom" the cult was to be utilized. The question was whether the cult was to become the monopoly of a Party elite manipulated for its own ends, and with Mao reduced to a figurehead on a pedestal, or was to be utilized by Mao Tse-tung and his dedicated true believers to popularize Mao's teachings as a means to "arm the people" with ideological weapons with which to act politically against, and seize power from, what Mao saw as usurpers led by privileged, reactionary, and even counterrevolutionary groups amounting to a "new class."

Emotions, personal and group loyalties and rivalries, individual and national self-esteem identified with Mao's charisma, were subjective factors so intermingled with the objective realities which opened the great schism that some foreign observers concluded there was no more to it than a palace squabble.

[1] *People's Daily*, Peking, May 5, 1967.

[2] Italics added. An untitled anthology of Mao Tse-tung's writings published by the Red Guards and generally accepted as authentic contains a "Draft Revolution from the Office of the Center of the C.C.P., Sixty Points on Working Methods," dated January 31, 1958. First translated in "Current Background," American Consulate General, Hongkong (No. 892, October 21, 1969), and later reissued by the U. S. State Department. The version here is from Jerome Ch'en, *Mao Papers, Anthology and Bibliography* (London, 1970), pages 65–66.

Perhaps it was China's equivalent of a general election? In reality the cultural revolution's attacks on the Party and state superstructure posed two Chairmen—and two charismas—against each other, in a nation that could support only one President at a time. There was the prestige of bureaucratic office personified by Liu Shao-ch'i as constitutionally elected chief of state, head of the National Defense Council, and powerful organizer of the Party administrative structure. Supposedly in synthesis with that superstructure but actually in growing contradiction, there was Mao the hero image, ideological mentor, father figure of the revolution, leader of the Party, and *de facto* chieftain of the armed forces through his hold over the Party Military Affairs Commission.

That a true revolution occurred was evident when Mao's offensive led to internal struggle which caused a partial halt to the work of many branches of the Party and near-dissolution of the state superstructure. In the rebuilding process it became necessary to rewrite both the Party and the state constitutions, to confront reality frankly by eliminating pretensions to an independent state superstructure—pretensions still inherent in the constitution of the U.S.S.R.'s Supreme Soviet, on which the constitution of the National People's Congress of China had been modeled—despite glaring evidence of an omnipresent dictatorship by a Party claiming monopoly representation of the proletariat.[3]

I have mentioned that Chairman Mao fixed the date of his final break with Liu Shao-ch'i as January, 1965—but that preparations for such an eventuality began in 1959 or earlier. As it was in that same January, 1965, that I had first raised with the Chairman the question of a personality cult in China, the reason why I did so may here be relevant.

[3] For text of the 1969 Party Constitution, see Appendix. As of early 1972 the draft state constitution had not yet been approved by the National People's Congress.

In the autumn of 1964 and early winter of 1965, when I was in China again for the first time in five years, I was much struck by changes for the better in nearly every place I revisited. In 1959 the ideological fissures between China and Russia had widened to a chasm when Khrushchev reneged on his promise to give China a "sample atom bomb" and then in 1960 withdrew all Soviet technical advisers and canceled hundreds of contracts vital to China's industrialization. Some excesses during the Great Leap Forward and initial stages of the communes (1958-59), accompanied by self-deception and error, aggravated costly letdowns in production. Unprecedentedly bad weather and poor harvests also contributed to near-famine conditions until 1963.

By 1964-65 the economy had about recovered equilibrium, however. The "hardship years" of 1959-62 were past, food was relatively plentiful, and consumer essentials and services were more widely available. Industry was beginning to make up its losses and collective agriculture seemed to be working well. Relaxation and optimism apparently prevailed except for a gathering fear of war with the United States, spreading up from Vietnam.

The country seemed politically united behind Mao Tse-tung as never before.

"Only one thing puzzles me in the picture," I said to two old friends with whom I dined alone not long before I left. "That is what seems to me an immoderate glorification of Mao Tse-tung." Giant portraits of him now hung in the streets, busts were in every chamber, his books and photographs were everywhere on display to the exclusion of others. In the four-hour revolutionary pageant of dance and song, *The East Is Red,* Mao was the only hero. As a climax in that performance—presented, with a cast of 2,000, for the visiting King Mohammed Zahir Shah and the Queen of Afghanistan, accompanied by their host, Chairman Liu Shao-ch'i—I saw a portrait copied from a photograph taken by myself in 1936, blown up to about thirty feet high. It gave me a mixed feeling of pride of craftsmanship and uneasy recollection of similar extravaganzas of worship of Joseph Stalin seen during wartime years in Russia.

Portraits of Liu Shao-ch'i, Chou En-lai, P'eng Chen, Teng Hsiao-p'ing, and other Politburo leaders were still to be seen in offices and institutions, however, and the works of Liu were everywhere on sale. The one-man cult was not yet universal, but the trend was unmistakable.

My hosts were Kung P'eng,[4] a graduate of Yenching University, and her husband, Ch'iao Kuan-hua, then both vice-ministers of foreign affairs. I continued: "The extent of these displays is the only thing that makes me wonder whether the Chairman has enemies here. Surely everyone knows that he is the main author of the revolution, surely he does not personally need this form of exaggerated adulation? Is it really necessary?"

Kung P'eng smiled understandingly. "I know that many foreigners feel that way," she said. "Let me tell you a story. During the early years of the revolution there was a strange thing. When the peasants came to the October anniversary and went past the reviewing stand, many did the *k'ou-t'ou* before Chairman Mao. We had to keep guards posted there to prevent them from prostrating themselves. It takes time to make people understand that Chairman Mao is not an emperor or a god but a man who wants the peasants to stand up like men. Does that help you see to what excesses some people would go—and how very mild a kind of respect for the Chairman is being permitted?"

It did help to recall China's three thousand years of emperor worship, and I thanked her. All the same I asked the Chairman[5] when I saw him: "In the Soviet Union China has been criticized for fostering a cult of personality. Is there a basis for that?"

[4] A truly "high person" who died in 1970. See page 191 *n*.
[5] See Appendix, South of the Mountains to North of the Seas.

Mao replied that perhaps there was. It was said that Stalin had been the center of a cult of personality, and that Khrushchev had none at all. The Chinese people, critics said, had some (feelings or practices of this kind). There might be good reasons for some (more?). *Probably Mr. Khrushchev*, he concluded, *fell because he had no cult of personality at all.*

The implication was clear enough: Mao did have some enemies. At the same time he said that 95 percent of the people were for socialism and only 5 percent were opposed to him. Who were the 5 percent? I did not (nor did most Chinese) know them to be led by the man designated as Mao's successor, and to include about half the Politburo. Some evidence was there for those who knew how to interpret it, but Politburo solidarity still closely guarded most of the cracks in unity from the view of outsiders.

To return now to a few remarks made by the Chairman when I met him at the 1970 October parade.

I had been criticized, he said, for some things I had written, but he had read excerpts and he did not see anything harmful in them. They did not expect everyone to agree with them on every subject and I was right to keep an independent point of view. As for what I had written about the so-called personality cult, there was such a thing, why not write about it?

When he invited me to breakfast on December 18 the Chairman again brought up the subject. He was in favor of scientific investigators (of social phenomena), he said: Darwin, Kant, some American scientists, especially Lewis Henry Morgan, who studied primitive society, and whose works were well liked by Marx and Engels. Morgan's research on the Iroquois Indians and the origins of tribal religion and "the need to worship" lent support to historical materialism and concepts of class struggle, Mao said. From earlier conversations with the Chairman I knew that he had pondered long over man's yearning for belief in God or gods or their equivalent and—apart from sharing the Marx-Engels atheism in the matter—had derived political lessons of his own from such study.

Later on he reminded me that he had told me in 1965 that there was some worship of the individual but that there was need for some more. At that time the power of the Party had been out of his control.

But now things were different, he said. It (the cult) had been overdone, there was a lot of formalism. For example, the so-called "four greats": that is, Great Teacher, Great Leader, Great Supreme Commander, Great Helmsman. What a nuisance! They would all be dispensed with sooner or later. Only the word "teacher" would be retained: that is, schoolteacher. He had always been a schoolteacher and still was one. The rest would be declined.

II

The Culture

But what *was* the teacher seeking to teach that had not been getting through to the masses? What was the important content beyond the form of the busts and portraits paraded by the perhaps "insincere" Party Propaganda Department which had fallen out of the Chairman's control?

Four large volumes of the *Selected Works of Mao Tse-tung,* another volume of *Selected Works* not yet formally published but in circulation in the Party, and countless miscellaneous statements and reports were the basis of the teachings. But the briefest answer is the one put forward when the cultural revolution was launched on August 8, 1966, by the Eleventh Plenum of the Central Committee (Eighth Congress) as the final point of its sixteen-point program:

> In the great proletarian Cultural Revolution, it is imperative to hold aloft the great red banner of Mao Tse-tung's thought and put proletarian politics in command. . . . Mao Tse-tung's thought should be taken as the guide for action in the cultural revolution.
>
> . . . Party committees at all levels must study and apply Chairman Mao's works all the more conscientiously and in a creative way. In particular, they must study over and

over again Chairman Mao's writings on the cultural revolution and on the Party's methods of leadership, such as *On the New Democracy, Talks at the Yenan Forum on Literature and Art, On the Correct Handling of Contradictions Among the People, Speech at the Chinese Communist Party's National Conference on Propaganda Work, Some Questions Concerning Methods of Leadership, and Methods of Work of Party Committees.*[1] . . .

To summarize the teacher's teachings—which embrace a historical outline of the Party and the revolution—is a very difficult task. It was done by defense chief Lin Piao, who compiled what became known everywhere as the "little red book" of Mao's Quotations. Lin began it in 1962 by publishing in the People's Liberation Army newspaper, *Chieh-fang-chun Pao (Liberation Daily)*—one organ that had remained all-Mao—a quotation a day. In 1964 he brought the most cogent pieces (some are lengthy excerpts, some even entire) into convenient pocket-book size suitable for every soldier's pack and had it memorized by all—to thoroughly indoctrinate the army, to saturate the vast peasantry, and finally, in 1966, to flood the cities. Literally hundreds of millions rolled out and eventually appeared in every significant language of the world.

"Three constantly read articles" in the book give a fair sampling in their simplest form of the lessons Mao sought to implant in every Chinese mind.

"Serving the People" is about an ordinary soldier who "died for the people" in a "worthy death," and Mao's eulogy on the occasion (1944) when he began the custom of holding a memorial meeting for every comrade who died, "be he soldier or cook," to honor the dead who serve—and so "unite all the people." *(Serving the people.)*

Another eulogy (1939), "In Memory of Dr. Norman Bethune," the Canadian doctor who died in the service of

[1] For complete text see Appendix, Resolutions of the Eleventh Plenum of the Central Committee—The Sixteen-Point Program.

the Chinese revolution, extols Bethune's "utter devotion to others," from which "every Communist must learn." He was a man "noble-minded and pure" and of "value to the people," his "spirit of internationalism" a glowing example of mutual support among all proletarians. (*Internationalism.*)

A third article, "The Foolish Old Man Who Removed the Mountains," based on a Chinese myth, tells of a farmer who attempted the impossible: to hoe down, with his two sons, two mountains which hemmed in his house. Ridiculed by wise men, he persisted, saying that more generations and more sons of the future would carry on the work they were beginning, and eventually they would succeed. And so, in the myth, they did—with the help of the gods. Mao likened the two peaks to the twin evils acting as dead weights on China—feudalism and imperialism—while the "gods" were "the masses," who, "digging together," would rid China of both incubuses.

Written in 1945, "The Old Man" contains serious political lessons, including a warning to prepare for American imperialism's help to Chiang Kai-shek but "to draw a distinction" between the people of the United States and their government, still a familiar theme today. (*Self-Reliance and Arduous Struggle.*)

Such homely examples give the tone of ingenuous boy scout virtue teaching which has always characterized Chinese Communist propaganda to combat "old habits, old customs, old ideas, and old culture" (Chinese and foreign bourgeois) of family and self first and community last. Beyond that, the mass propagation of a standard doctrinal method of objective reasoning, used to analyze and "sum up" concrete problems in a systematic, unified way, was to be achieved by the hard study of the foremost of Mao's cogent theoretical works, notably *On Contradiction, On Practice,* and *On the Correct Handling of Contradictions Among the People.*

If I seem to have drifted far from the cultural revolution story itself it is because its "origins" cannot be grasped by mere chronological recapitulation alone and without some side trips to see something of the "nature" of the "thoughts" that Mao's leadership sought and seeks to implant.

Was Liu Shao-ch'i, then, opposed to such virtues and homilies as exemplified in the three articles just synopsized? Certainly not. The Mao-Liu showdown came about because under Liu the Party was following a pragmatic policy, a policy of *yu-ming wu-shih* (having the name without the reality), in failing to integrate Mao's ideology with the daily life of the people. Liu strove to satisfy Mao just enough to preserve unity, while protecting and strengthening his organization against interference in carrying out practical administrative tasks in a systematic, albeit pedestrian, uninspired, and bureaucratic way.

Liu and Mao were very different in working style and temperament. Seven years Mao's junior, Liu was born in Mao's Hunan province; both studied, in the same normal school, to be teachers, but their conceptions of teaching were very far apart. Both came from rich-peasant families but Mao rebelled against his father, Liu did not. Both joined the Party in 1921, but Liu joined in Moscow (recruited from China by the Comintern), while Mao became a founder of the indigenous Party set up in Shanghai.

Liu was not pro-Russian but his early years in Russia influenced him; Mao learned about revolution by recruiting peasant guerrillas. Liu did not care for peasant life; he preferred underground conspiracy work in the cities and was a skillful organizer of workers and intellectuals. He tended to see results emerging less from zeal and exhortation than from the efforts of a professional human machine, a coordinated staff.

Mao disliked and distrusted city life, spent most of his pre-1949 days as a warrior politician, was contemptuous of "experts" and intellectuals who had never fired a gun or dug a field, respected the poor peasants who made his best soldiers, sought to champion and protect from urban corruption the "new workers" drawn largely from the ranks of the rural proletariat, and was exalted by armed struggle. He drew youthful disciples to him by appeals to their self-belief, idealism, and patriotism, as he drew themes for his poetry from a mixture of history glorified, classical allusions to man's struggle to tame nature, and man seen as "becoming god."

In a time when China was in transition from a predominantly agricultural to a predominantly industrial society the two men, in their very apposites, seemed ideally to complement each other. Indeed that seemed still to be the case when, in 1958, Mao resigned the chairmanship of the People's Republic in favor of Liu and (it was said) in order to devote full time to Party affairs. In that year he bequeathed to the Party the remarkable document called "Sixty Points on Working Methods," in which he commented, "The important points (on rules and regulations) are drafted by Comrade Liu Shao-ch'i after consultations with comrades working in the regions."[2]

For one thing, the timing and manner of the split with Russia, and differences of opinion over that, began to break the rhythm of the Mao-Liu tandem from 1959 onward. The Sino-Russian disease had begun to pustulate at the Moscow Conference of 1957; its ravages became world-evident after Khrushchev's visit to Camp David in 1959, following his June withdrawal of the promise of atom bombs to China. In September, the same month Khrushchev visited Eisenhower—a visit Mao viewed with considerable suspicion—P'eng Teh-huai was dismissed from his post as defense minister.

That followed the decisive plenum of the Central Committee held at Lushan, where P'eng had defied Mao and Mao had had to throw all his prestige behind the debate to win the vote of censure against P'eng.

[2] Jerome Ch'en, *Mao Papers, op. cit.*, page 57.

Who was P'eng Teh-huai? No relation to Peking mayor P'eng Chen—whose career was urban-oriented—P'eng Teh-huai was a rough-and-ready warrior of peasant origin who had but two years of classroom study. Born in 1899, in the same county of Hunan province as Mao, he ran away from tyranny in his peasant home, became a derelict and then, in his early teens, a soldier. In 1928 he was in command of a Nationalist regiment when he led an uprising and took his men to join Mao Tse-tung's guerrillas. Thereafter he supported Mao, who was his political tutor. P'eng made (and repeatedly admitted) many mistakes in battle and ideology but he became an able tactician and Mao trusted and liked him. P'eng owed his rapid rise above others in the army chiefly to Mao's confidence in him.

In Korea, except for a brief initial phase of command by Lin Piao, P'eng was leader of the Chinese "volunteers." As such he became a national hero and was elevated to the rank of field marshal, defense minister, and chief of the P.L.A. While working closely with the Russians in Korea he was impressed by Soviet logistics and aid in modernizing China's military industries. In 1959 he visited Russia and Eastern Europe on a long tour, during which he met Khrushchev just before the latter's "fatal" trip to Camp David. Propaganda attacks later accused him of delivering a letter to Mr. K. criticizing Mao's leadership, but the letter has yet to be produced.

What was beyond doubt was that on his return to China to appear at the Lushan conference, he brashly attacked the Party's failures under Mao and inferentially blamed Mao for heavy losses caused by the Great Leap Forward, the people's communes, the "general line," and the split with Russia. He also seriously questioned exaggerated claims being made for results of campaigns such as "backyard" steel production, an experiment he asserted had cost China a billion dollars. Among P'eng's sympathizers were his own chief of staff, Huang K'eh-ch'eng, and the former

Party general secretary, Chang Wen-t'ien, an old Mao adversary.

When I first met P'eng Teh-huai in 1936 he was deputy commander of the First Front Red Army—blunt, tough, a man of boundless energy and revolutionary enthusiasm but short on Marxist training. He could never have become Mao's intellectual match; in 1959 he was easily outwitted and, seemingly humbled, admitted his mistakes and apologized. Having regarded P'eng's major virtues as courage and loyalty to his chief's military and political strategy and tactics, Mao must have felt his defection as a very severe personal disappointment. Although P'eng was dropped from the Politburo he remained on the Central Committee. He said he would retire "to do farm work."

Allegedly encouraged by Liu Shao-ch'i to persevere, however, P'eng found time in 1960-61 to travel and write five "reports on field investigations" which amounted to further opposition to Mao's leadership. These were circulated to Central Committee members. At the Tenth Plenary Session of the Central Committee, in September, 1962, P'eng produced an 80,000-word document which repeated and greatly enlarged his criticisms. This time he was probably supported by Liu Shao-ch'i and Party general secretary Teng Hsiao-p'ing, who sought a "rejudgment and reinstatement" for P'eng.

Two other facts must be kept in mind to which some allusion has already been made. Those in the army who covertly backed P'eng—sometimes called "the professionals"—favored at least a temporary compromise with Russia. They wanted Russian help to complete the technological modernization of the army, including access to the Bomb. They could get that only by taking a junior position in an alliance on unequal terms—like the satellites in the Warsaw Pact—to which Mao was unalterably opposed. They had another motive, which is the second fact of significance.

Continuation of Russian arms aid meant continuation of close liaison between army administrators and the Russian army command on an operational level. That in turn meant creation of a "professional clique" or group in China able to utilize dependence on Russia to counter and limit the sovereign power exercised chiefly by Mao. They wanted an army of professional officers modeled along Russian lines, freed from nonmilitary production and army-to-people tasks, and closely tied to the professional bureaucracy. They wanted to break Mao's grip on the army and use their "independence" from him to curb or control the cult of personality and to determine military policy.

That P'eng had supporters in the Party propaganda machine was evident when a popular movie, *Wave of Anger*, and a novel, *Defense of Yenan*, appeared in the 1950s with thinly veiled glorification of P'eng and corresponding diminishment of Mao. Both film and book were to be exhumed and vilified along with later literary products such as *Hai Jui Dismissed from Office*, when the cultural revolution began to "bombard the headquarters" of Liu Shao-ch'i, to whose side of the dispute this account may now revert.

Before 1962, Liu Shao-ch'i had never overtly opposed Mao personally. At Lushan he accepted, if lukewarmly, the choice of Lin Piao to replace P'eng. In his published articles and speeches of 1959-60 Liu staunchly defended Mao's supreme leadership—and praised the communes, the Great Leap, and the "general line." In December, 1960, however, there appeared one oddly anachronistic note in a speech published during his visit to Moscow, months after the decisive Mao-Khrushchev break. In ten publicly reported speeches he made in Russia he failed to offer any salute to Mao's leadership except once. Then he quoted Mao in a context from which, curiously, he drew the inference that Mao wished to "follow the path of the Russians." To that he added, "My personal experience has also proved this." From 1961 to 1966, in China and during travels in Korea, Pakistan, Southeast Asia, and Indonesia, Liu made only an occasional token reference to Chairman Mao.

Meanwhile, in 1960 and 1961, the Central Committee had been obliged to make a temporary retreat on its road to socialism—something like the New Economic Policy of Lenin's day. "Serving agriculture first" took priority over heavy industry, basic ownership of the land went to the commune village (cooperative), family ownership of farm homes and small private plots was guaranteed, and limited free markets were permitted, while the bonus system and other material incentives were introduced in industry. It was a time for the pragmatist (or opportunist) and a trend toward Libermanism—in China called "economism"—with newly rich peasants reaching for kulak status.

Mao's "three red banners"—the people's communes, the Great Leap Forward, and the "general line" (of constructing socialism) were criticized by Liu in 1962, in Party meetings of which the reports were not, of course, openly published before the cultural revolution. In the same year a *public* event of great importance took place—whose significance was, once more, totally lost on the host of foreign "China watchers." The Party Propaganda Department, headed by Politburo member Lu Ting-yi, ordered reprinted, in large numbers, Liu Shao-ch'i's book *On Self-Cultivation of Communists*.[3]

---

[3] Widely used in indoctrination courses for Communist Youth League members and also senior cadres; translated into English as *How to Be a Good Communist* (Foreign Languages Press, Peking, 1951). Liu's *On Inner Party Struggle* and *On Internationalism and Nationalism* (both F.L.P., 1951) were catechismal texts used at all levels of Party schools before the cultural revolution.

12

Conspiracy by Propaganda

When *On Self-Cultivation of Communists* first appeared in Yenan, in 1939, Communists were a small minority of the people, seeking to win over wavering intellectuals, petit bourgeois, and national bourgeois elements to their leadership in the Patriotic War Against Japan. *Self-Cultivation* minimized class struggle and stressed the importance of discipline and self-criticism, suggesting that being a Communist depended on a virtuous mental outlook attainable by anyone. *Hsiu-yang*, or "self-cultivation," had Confucian derivations and implications of "class harmony" as a Communist ideal.

Intended to fit the united-front period, it contained anachronisms hardly suitable for the 1960s, when proletarian dictatorship prevailed and China was competing with Russia for ideological leadership of world revolution. Liu Shao-ch'i made some additions and deletions but the emphasis and content remained the same. What was wrong with it? In an important passage quoting Lenin, for example, Liu unaccountably deleted the sentence, "The dictatorship of the proletariat means a persistent struggle—bloody and bloodless, violent and peaceful,

military and economic, educational and administrative—
against the traditions of the old society." More enigmatically, the 1962 edition still omitted the words here
italicized in the following sentence: "All these reasons
make *the dictatorship of the proletariat necessary and*
victory over the bourgeoise impossible without a long,
stubborn and desperate life-and-death struggle . . ."

Throughout *Self-Cultivation,* essentially a moralistic
essay preaching high ethics for individual perfection, Liu
failed to integrate his message with lessons of the Mao
doctrine of "people's war" against feudalism and imperialism, and of armed struggle as basic to the seizure of
power by the proletariat. Above all, he wholly ignored
important wartime and postwar works of Mao Tse-tung
such as *On the People's Democratic Dictatorship* and
*On the Correct Handling of Contradictions Among the
People.*

While the foregoing points were stressed in vituperative
polemics later conducted against Liu, his book contained
other passages which suggested support for P'eng Teh-
huai and opposition to Chairman Mao's leadership.
Within the Party, Liu declared:

> We had certain representatives of dogmatism who at one
> time were even worse . . . regarded themselves as "China's
> Marx" or "China's Lenin" and had the impudence to
> require that our Party members should revere them as
> Marx and Lenin were revered, support them as "the
> leaders" and accord them loyalty and devotion . . . And
> indeed they were discarded by our Party members. But
> can we say with full confidence that no such people will
> reappear in our Party? No, we cannot say so . . . No mem-
> ber of our Party has any right to demand that the rank and
> file should support or keep him as a leader.

In its original meaning Liu's criticism was clearly aimed
at former rivals of Mao, Party strong men such as Wang
Ming and Li Li-san, who had been discredited and

LEFT TO RIGHT FROM TOP:
Chou En-lai greeting Edgar Snow, Shensi, 1936 / "Saturday Brigades"
—Red Army youth working in the countryside, 1936 / The Chinese
Red Army of the 1930s / "Little Red Devils" studying, 1936

A day's work at Nanniwan (see Chapter 17)

Nanniwan: Right, Chu Shao-ching. Left, Long March veteran Wang Ming-teh, who remembers being treated by Dr. Norman Bethune

The May Seventh School at Nanniwan

A co-op store in Yellow
Ridge commune

Sian: Nineteenth Cereal
Store

A housewives' commune
—self-started—in
Liaoning (Northeast China)

English-language students, Peking

Dr. Lin Ch'iao-chih (see Chapter 5) showing stages of gestation in plastic models

ABOVE: *A rural school in Hopei province* BELOW: *A student drama group (No. 31 Middle School, Peking) entertains in the school yard*

Sunday afternoon at the Great Wall, outside Peking

Winter Palace, Peking

overthrown. The book contained many other passages of possible *double entendre*. Why did Liu reprint them—when he deleted other anachronistic material—just in August, 1962, when P'eng was circulating his 80,000-word critique, with Liu's knowledge?

At the same time Liu had his *Self-Cultivation* (50,000 words) printed again in the *People's Daily* and *Red Flag* (the Party theoretical organ) and put into wide use. And why did Lo Jui-ch'ing, P.L.A. chief of staff, arrange to distribute Liu's book for army teaching material just at the moment when Lin Piao, his superior, was striving to unify ideological training by mass use of primers of the Thought of Mao Tse-tung? Was the Party, if not Mao himself, grooming Liu to supersede Mao's teachings as well as Mao himself? Liu did seem to be building up a revisionist school of rival propaganda. In any case that was to become the general theme of a cacophonous orchestration of ideological attacks launched against "China's Khrushchev" in 1967.

One more revelatory human and political note. From 1961 onward Liu and Mao were often separated when for long periods Mao absented himself from Peking—as was his habit—to visit the countryside and the army. Some important decisions taken at Politburo meetings and Party "work conferences" were implemented without consulting him. Mao later complained about Teng Hsiao-p'ing, general secretary and member of the five-man Politburo Standing Committee, as follows: "Teng Hsiao-p'ing is deaf [hard of hearing] but at meetings he would sit far away from me. In the six years since 1959 he has not reported to me about his work. He relies only on P'eng Chen for the work of the secretariat."[1]

---

[1] According to Red Guard literature: *Chairman Mao's Selected Writings*, "Speech at C. C. Political Work Report Meeting (24 Oct., 1966)" (Joint Publishing Research Service, 49826, Feb. 12, 1970, Washington, D. C.), p. 12.

Among important items Teng Hsiao-p'ing may have failed to report to Mao was a policy abbreviated in Chinese as *san tzu yi-pao* (three freedoms and one contract), meaning: "the extension of plots for private use and of free markets, the increase of small enterprises with sole responsibility for their own profits and losses, and the fixing of output quotas [in communes] based on the household [individual enterprise]." Its implications tended toward adoption of "economism" and revisionism, and directly contradicted the Socialist Education Movement, which eventually suppressed it as part of the "four cleanups," that is: socialist rectification in the fields of politics, ideology, organization, and economy.

The economy recovered by 1964 and the neopragmatist cadres sought to preserve and enlarge material incentives. They were opposed by Mao, with help from the army, in a counterattack which began in the army and the countryside as the Socialist Education Movement. The S.E.M. program was later on much radicalized, to become the basis of the sixteen-point manifesto of the cultural revolution finally proclaimed in August, 1966.[2] Meanwhile Lin Piao built up, through the General Political Department—the ruling Party section of the P.L.A.—a corps of about one million Maoist "activists." They took a leading part in the crackdown on those in the countryside suffering from a "spontaneous desire to become capitalists." The drift toward revisionism was arrested in the communes, with the poor and middle peasant majority used to put down the get-rich-quick mentality of peasant opportunists. Now it was the city's turn.

Why "cultural" revolution? It was so named because its initial thrust was against propaganda (cultural) leaders in the Party who were said to be following a bourgeois or "capitalist road" and undermining Maoist ideology. In the

[2] For complete text see Appendix, Resolutions of the Eleventh Plenum of the Central Committee—The Sixteen-Point Program.

early 1960s attacks on Mao's leadership had begun surreptitiously in the arts and the press, where there were now increasingly open critical-allegorical references to the Chairman.

Singled out as the foremost "demon" and "monster" at the outset, late in 1965, was Wu Han, one of six deputy mayors of Peking and a close friend of Mayor P'eng Chen. A trade union product and protégé of Liu Shao-ch'i, P'eng Chen was the dominant Politburo member in North China. Wu Han was a professional historian and rather prolific writer who specialized in the Ming period. I had known him as a bourgeois liberal historian. He never became a Party member but supported the Communists against Chiang Kai-shek. Now he wrote a number of pieces in praise of his favorite historical figure, Hai Jui, an upright model bureaucrat of the Ming Dynasty who had dared to criticize the emperor and was unjustly punished. *Hai Jui Scolds the Emperor* was Wu's first play, and the sequel to it, *Hai Jui Dismissed from Office*, was produced with success in 1961.

Emboldened by background support from puissant figures in the hierarchy, Wu—a "docile tool"?—had also joined others in writing, in Aesopian language, a long series of newspaper essays under such titles as *Evening Chats at Yenshan* and *Three-Family Village*.[3] Wu's two close collaborators were Teng T'o, a cultural acolyte of P'eng Chen, and Liao Mo-sha, P'eng's expert on united-front work. The trio wrote under a joint pen name. Their work could not have been published without the tacit support of Lu Ting-yi, the Politburo member in charge of propaganda, and his deputy, Chou Yang, also a Central Committee member.

The cleverness at dissimulation of Wu Han, Teng T'o, and Liao Mo-sha did not hide from sophisticated inner

[3] In the form of dialogues between villagers and intellectuals, these essays indirectly attacked, by use of myths or historical anecdotes, the "three red banners" or main socialist line of Mao.

Party circles their double intention in recounting seem-ingly innocuous historical anecdotes and fables, to satirize and ridicule Mao and the "three red banners." So it was later alleged, although no single China specialist, including Chinese, drew such analogies at the time. Why had Mao done nothing to suppress the tales as they had spun on through 1961 to 1963?

Whether it was Wu Han's quixotic intention really to cross swords with Mao or not, there was no doubt how some Party leaders interpreted *Hai Jui Dismissed from Office*. To them it reflected a war of attrition against Mao's power, covertly led by P'eng Chen. Was Liu Shao-ch'i fully behind P'eng Chen? He later denied it. "The crux of the dismissal of Hai Jui lies in the dismissal itself," Mao wrote in 1965. "Emperor Chia Ch'ing dismissed Hai Jui; in 1959 we sacked P'eng Teh-huai. P'eng *is* Hai Jui."[4] But Mao said that only in 1967; it would not have done for him crudely to open the assault himself, in 1965. Who would do the job for him?

A fact which helped convince Mao that no less than a second revolution to overthrow some top Party leaders was required to get the whole nation firmly back on his revolutionary road—which he saw as the only road—was that he could not find any appropriate Party person in the North, nor any intellectuals either, to expose Wu Han, sheltered as he was by the mighty. He had to go to Shanghai to find his man: Yao Wen-yuan, a relatively young writer who in 1957 had won Mao's praise for an able polemic against bourgeois outcroppings in the arts and journalism. Rather, it was Chiang Ch'ing (Mme. Mao Tse-tung) who consulted Yao Wen-yuan, an old friend of hers. She herself was by 1965 very active in a struggle against Wu Han and pro-Liu Party people in Shanghai opposed to her ideas of new dramas, operas, and ballets with a

---

[4] In a statement described as a self-criticism P'eng Teh-huai him-self later admitted that he was intended to be Hai Jui.

proletarian content: plays to be true to Mao's ideas about art for the masses, and plays strongly opposed by the Peking cultural propaganda apparatus.

It was Yao Wen-yuan who drafted the critique of *Hai Jui* and Wu Han. Revised eleven times, we are told, and seen by both Chiang Ch'ing and Mao, it was finally published in November in Shanghai—because, as we have seen, Mao could not at first get the Party press in Peking to use it.

Yao's article charged Wu Han with grave *ideological* errors, such as idealizing a feudal personality while ignoring the main class struggle of the masses against the emperor, the bureaucrats, and the landlords. The limit of Hai Jui's "reform" demand was to return half of the land seized by high officials to the original landlords, so as to safeguard the stability of "the system." Rapidly other articles became more specific, to reach ever higher in counterattacks on those in charge of the propaganda machine, persons as yet unnamed except for Wu Han.

Now under serious pressure, P'eng Chen sought a way out for Wu Han, whose dilemma became his own. He would be held responsible if Wu and other close allies were declared ideological enemies, and akin to counterrevolutionaries. P'eng Chen was a member of a Group of Five in Charge of the Cultural Revolution secretly set up by the Central Committee in October, 1965. In the name of the Group P'eng circulated a telegram, in February, 1966, to all party branches which attempted to minimize Wu Han's offense as a mere "academic" error. At the same time his report slighted the main aims of the cultural revolution, already clearly defined by Mao as the removal of "top Party persons in authority who are taking the capitalist road." Instead, P'eng called for a movement confined to criticisms to be conducted "with the approval of the leading [Party] bodies concerned."

Mao charged that P'eng's telegram had not been seen by other members of the Group of Five, nor by Mao him-

self. Enraged, the Chairman called a special meeting of
the Central Committee and had P'eng's report completely
repudiated. That was on May 16, 1966. So devastating was
the Central Committee's May 16 Circular Telegram that
it put P'eng foremost among "those representatives of the
bourgeoisie who have sneaked into the party, the government, the army, and various cultural circles." In other
words, a counterrevolutionary. Ominously the Circular
concluded:

> Once conditons are ripe, they will seize political power
> and turn the dictatorship of the proletariat into a dic-
> tatorship of the bourgeoisie. Some of them we have
> already seen through, others we have not. Some are still
> trusted by us and are being trained as our successors,
> persons like Khrushchev, for example, who are still nes-
> tling beside us.[5]

From then on it was "civil war without guns"—more
or less!

[5] Jerome Ch'en, *op. cit.*, pages 112–13.

13
Open Warfare

From the autumn of 1965 Mao had remained lost to public view, nor did the May 16, 1966, meeting and communiqué disclose his whereabouts; both were to remain Party secrets until the following year. Evidently Mao's movements were known only to members of the small Cultural Revolution Group in the Central Committee which had replaced P'eng Chen's Group. An impression spread that Mao was ill or convalescing.

It is possible that I unwittingly contributed to that impression. In his interview with me in January, 1965, the Chairman seemed somewhat less than his usual robust self. Twice he enigmatically remarked that he was "soon going to see God,"[1] and some other comments suggested a readiness to leave the future to his "successors," which was hardly indicative of preparations for a great struggle just ahead. Later I was told in Peking that such remarks to me may have been intended to mislead his enemies—to encourage them to expose themselves further while the strategy of an offensive was being laid. That is mere surmise, however.

In fact, Mao secretly visited Shanghai in November and talked to young and future vanguard Party rebels of the

[1] See Appendix, South of the Mountains to North of the Seas.

cultural revolution such as Yao Wen-yuan and Chang Ch'un-ch'iao, who were soon to organize and lead a rebellion to overthrow Liu's henchmen in charge of the Party, labor unions, and cultural institutions there. Far from being an invalid, Mao was busy traveling in the South, issuing directives. In the North, the Central Committee's Group prepared a *coup de grâce* for P'eng and for the "No. 1 Party person in authority taking the capitalist road," as yet not publicly named. At the Tenth Plenary Session of the Central Committee, in 1962, Mao had said, *"To overthrow a political power it is always necessary first of all to create public opinion, to do work in the ideological sphere. That is true for the revolutionary class as well as for the counter-revolutionary class."*

Yao Wen-yuan's critique of Wu Han had appeared in the unofficial press[2] of Shanghai at a time when the official Party press there and in Peking, except for P.L.A. organs, was still outside Mao's control. In June, 1966, the army paper in Peking took over the *People's Daily*, official organ of the Central Committee, and *Hung-ch'i*, the theoretical journal of the Party Center.[3] It announced a "sharp class struggle" to eliminate the "black anti-Party line" and to promote proletarian ideology in education, literature, journalism, the theater, and other cultural activities.

On June 3 the *People's Daily* published a "decision of the Central Committee" to fire the *Daily's* former editorial board. The same decision declared that the Peking Party Committee had been "reorganized under Li Hsueh-feng, Long March veteran, Politburo member, and Minister of Public Security. P'eng Chen's name was not mentioned but from that time on he was eliminated from all official and Party positions. Into the political limbo with him went Wu Han and all P'eng's "academic" allies. Another dictum

[2] *Wen Hui Pao (Evening News).*

[3] The "Center" means the Central Committee of the Party, and in particular the Standing Committee of the Politburo, which serves as its inner executive authority.

of great importance ordered the dismissal of Lu P'ing and P'eng P'ei-yuan from their leadership of Peking University. The Party committee they headed was to be "reorganized" by a new "work team" selected by the new Peking Party Committee.

How such Central Committee decisions were reached, exactly who was present at the secret May 16 meeting, was not clear. Was attendance at such meetings carefully chosen or "beefed up" by alternate civilian and military members? Whether it was that Mao lacked a majority of the Central Committee necessary to overthrow the constitutionally elected head of the state, or whether he preferred it that way, he turned to the non-Party masses, to mobilize and indoctrinate millions of youths (the army was instructed to "support the left") to remove key anti-Mao bureaucrats ("revisionists") entrenched in political and academic seats of power.

The revolution to carry out the May 16 communiqué had by June unfolded everywhere, preparing for the Eleventh Plenary Session of the Central Committee summoned in August. Schools were closed, Red Guards began warring for control of all cultural institutions, and a wave of *ta tzu-pao* began to blanket the nation with wholesale accusations and revelations about "demons," "monsters," and "capitalist roaders."

As the storm mounted Mao Tse-tung resurfaced dramatically on July 16 at Wuhan, the great industrial city of Central China, to swim across the Yangtze River. He was accompanied by 5,000 "rebel revolutionaries" and a tremendous press and television coverage. The "only sun in our hearts," as the banners proclaimed him, was visibly in excellent health, full of battle, and ready to take full charge at the helm. He then triumphantly returned to Peking.

It did not seem that Liu Shao-ch'i made any planned serious attempt to meet Mao's challenge in all-out warfare, or even fully realized, before August, that he himself was the No. 1 target. That he aimed to erode Mao's power by reducing the cult to a façade behind which the Party power would be wielded by those who abided by the rules seems apparent enough. But was not the Party constitution clearly designed to prevent rule by the cult of the individual in favor of collective leadership?

> . . . our Party abhors the deification of the individual . . . The Central Committee has always been against . . . exaggerating the role of leaders in works and literature. Of course the cult of the individual is a social phenomenon with a long history and it cannot but find certain reflections in our Party and public life. It is our task to continue to observe faithfully the Central Committee's opposition to the elevation and glorification of the individual.[4]

Now this organizational man, Liu, the legalist and head of the Party Establishment, this firm believer in Party constitutionality, was probably temperamentally incapable of believing in the true extent of Mao's daring. Could his intention actually be to break up the Party machine itself —to Liu the life of the Party—to carry through a revolution by command of the cult? All Liu's previous experience with Mao's rectification movements had failed to prepare him for anything so drastic.

Who could have foreseen the Red Guards? Was there a word of sanction for them in the May 16 communiqué? Certainly not. They were illegal, thought Liu. Who could anticipate that the Party Founder would call upon the masses—not just the well-machined Young Communists, disciplined and "docile tools" trained in Liu's Party education programs, but the non-Party unruly multitudes— to rebel against the Establishment itself? Indeed, the rebels violated nearly every rule in the 1956 Party constitution— that document so closely modeled after the Russian prototype—on which Liu and General Secretary Teng Hsiao-

---

[4] *The Constitution of the Communist Party of China*, and Teng Hsiao-p'ing, "Report on the Revision . . ." Eighth National Congress of the C.C.P. (Foreign Languages Press, Peking, 1956).

p'ing had labored long and hard. Could they break the laws of the state constitution, to act illegally against the elected president of the National Congress? All this with Mao's benevolent approval? How could that be?

Not that Liu remained inactive. From May on his main effort was to preserve the Organization, which he and Teng had so painstakingly built up, from Mao's dangerously destructive course. Everywhere I heard the story from the lips of rebel participants it was the same. The Old Guard tried to meet the onslaught betimes by sending out hundreds of cadres in "work teams" to the schools, factories, institutes, to "lead" the revolution into innocuous channels, to prevent the breakup of Party nuclei and cells, and to discredit the "troublemakers."

But Mao's Cultural Revolution Group in the Central Committee had their own cadres at work too; at the start they were few but very determined. The Central Committee had ordered all classes dismissed for a revolutionization of the curriculum. Debate and free attacks on leadership were the order of the day, rebellion was justified, and so were big-character posters attacking authority.

The Red Guards appeared first in Peita (Peking University), late in May, and were promptly suppressed as "anti-Party" by Liu's "work teams." Exactly who started them was unknown. The general I met in Hangchow, very familiar with Mao's entire strategy during the cultural revolution, told me that they were one thing neither planned nor foreseen. Their potential was, however, quickly recognized by Mao. Encouraged, the Red Guards rose again at Peita, and spread elsewhere. They were suppressed again, and a seesaw struggle ensued. Then in June Mao proclaimed, "The Red Guards are good" and the nation saw a Red Guard explosion.

Statements of self-criticism later attributed to Liu Shao-ch'i may not be authentic but possess a certain lonely dignity and lack of excessive self-abasement which lend some plausibility to a number of points. One of them is that for the "first fifty days" after June 1, before Mao returned to Peking, Liu engaged in intensive efforts, through his work teams, to carry out what he understood to be the aims of the cultural revolution. He saw only in retrospect that he had been sabotaging the revolution by attempting to isolate the rebels and "oppose struggles to oust the cadres."

"I was," the statement reads, "gripped by the fear of confusion, ultrademocracy, and uprisings of counterrevolutionaries." Even after Mao's return, however, Liu continued personally to try to guide cadres and work teams because, he said, "prior to August 5," he still "did not understand [his] mistake in line and orientation" and "often aimed at maintaining the old order and opposing the revolutionary rebel spirit . . ."

And what happened on August 5? That was one week before the decisive eleventh session of the Central Committee which adopted the sixteen-point cultural revolution program and demoted Liu Shao-ch'i from second place in the hierarchy to No. 8. And August 5 was the day Mao Tse-tung wrote up his own big-character poster. Its contents—"*Bombard the Headquarters*"—immediately swept the land. Not long afterward Mao put a band on his sleeve and publicly joined the Red Guard revolutionary rebels. Between then and November he was to review, at the Heavenly Peace Gate, no fewer than eleven million youths from all over China engaged in the overthrow of the old Establishment.

On August 5 Liu recognized at last that he *was* "headquarters" when he read in the *People's Daily* the following lines by Mao:

Bombard the Headquarters—My Big-Character Poster

In the last 50 days or so some leading comrades from the central down to the local levels have . . . struck down the surging movement of the great Cultural Revolution of the proletariat. They have stood facts on their head and juggled black and white, encircled the suppressed revolutionaries, stifled opinions differing from their own, imposed a white terror, and felt very pleased with themselves.

"It was Chairman Mao and the Party Central Committee which asked me," wrote Liu, "to take charge of the work of the Central Committee when Chairman Mao is not in Peking," and that was how Liu found himself in those "fifty days" of trouble. How could he, without specific directives, know that he was supposed to abolish himself and the Party apparatus he headed? He could only act as he always had, and as Mao perhaps foresaw that he would act—"to preserve the cadres"—thereby entering a well-prepared trap. Perhaps he had been no less astonished than the rest of the country when the Chairman appeared, in mid-July, calmly swimming the Yangtze.

The battle was about over for Liu—if he had ever begun it, on Mao's terms—but it was not till the next year that he was identified as "China's Khrushchev" by name, in the press. And not until the autumn of 1968 was he expelled by the Central Committee and read out of the Party in high disgrace.

During those many months the revolution went from one stage to another as youth razed the old structure and the Group sought to lead them to seize power at every level and create something better. What Mao had thought would take about a year in the end took more than three. What was fully as surprising as Mao's leadership of a popular revolt against those in authority in the Party he had built was the stubborn resistance of the great machine to such massive attack. The vessel was more stoutly made than many had supposed—and the new ship was not to be completed in a day.

As already forecast, the foregoing summary is far from satisfactory as history. It is incomplete. We do not really hear from the defeated. It omits many important and modifying facts: poignant events such as the impact on the lives of old revolutionaries, and the rending of old loyalties which accompanied moments of real but limited civil war between factions that arose in every branch of society including the army. Where, for instance, is there room to fit Chou En-lai into the framework—the man who almost single-handedly held together the main energies of production and the administrative talent while the great turnover shook the nation?

That question, like so many others, may better be answered—if it can be only in small part—by moving the narrative from the recent past back to the present, into the relative calm after the storm.

Part Four

The Army, the Party, and the People

14

A Military Dictatorship?

All China is a great school of Mao Tse-tung Thought and the army is its headmaster. "We are all connected with the army," said Premier Chou En-lai, and he might have added, "The army connects all of us."

Premier Chou was patiently explaining to me why it is misleading to single out individuals in the rebuilt Party and government administration as "military" and "non-military." Is not Mao Tse-tung "military"? Father of the army, which he, with Chu Teh, organized and led at the beginning, he is also lifetime head of the Party. When Mao was chairman of the Republic (till 1958) he united in himself the Party-army-state trinity; as lifetime chairman of the Party's Military Affairs Commission he has been *de facto* commander-in-chief since 1935.

Chou En-lai himself was a general in command of the Eastern Front Army in Shensi when I first met him in 1936 in the old Chinese Red Army—before it became the People's Liberation Army. Lin Piao wore the stars of a marshal before he abolished insignia of rank in 1965.

In the beginning was the Word, and the Word was Party. But "without a people's army," Mao said, "the people have nothing," and neither had the Party. They grew together and were interdependent, "as the lips and teeth," as Chinese express it.

When I first saw the old Red Army bases in Northwest China during the civil war, the Party politico was usually indistinguishable, to an outsider, from the combat Communist. All wore the same blue or gray (depending on how faded) cotton uniform with no insignia of rank except a red tab on the collar lapel (as is again the case today), shared the same or similar quarters, ate about the same food as the peasants ate, and faced the same perils and hardships with minimal material incentives. Commissars often doubled as commanders and vice versa, learning from each other. That remained true throughout the Anti-Japanese War and the renewed civil war that followed.

With victory, in 1949, Mao Tse-tung said: "The army is a school. Our field armies of 2,100,000 are equivalent to several thousand universities and secondary schools. We have to rely chiefly on the army to supply our cadres."

It had taken twenty-two years of ceaseless . armed struggle to create that revolutionary "school"; civilian recruits had to absorb the experience vicariously. Much of the urban working class was then politically weak, and petty bourgeois in outlook. It was mainly the combat Communists, who were for the most part of peasant origin, who organized and indoctrinated proletarian cadres, reversing classical Marxist expectations.

The great buildup of the nonsoldier Party came rapidly after the Communists took over administrative responsibility for a nation of continental size. By 1956, when the People's Republic was only seven years old, Party membership reached ten million, of whom about 80 percent had joined after the revolution. In 1960 there were seventeen million, of whom 70 percent had joined after the Korean war. Membership by 1965 was said to approach eighteen million, plus some thirty million Young Communists. Party membership was still two-thirds peasant in origin, but among the administrators were many technicians and intellectuals of bourgeois origin. Except at high levels the Party *veterans* were a dwindling minority.

The army nevertheless was still the "great school" and ideological seedbed. With the militia, it contained a far larger concentration of senior Party cadres than any other single branch of public service.

Complex historical circumstances, thus far but dimly screened here, had created something more than a generation gap between veterans who traced back to the Long March or the Yenan days, on one "front," and those who came later, on another "front." In the relatively secure and partly "socialized" base sanctuary in Northwest China, where Mao worked out his ideological adaptations of Marxism to Chinese conditions, experience with the problems of landlord and bourgeois influence had been minimal as compared to that in East China, where recruits were trained in guerrilla areas tenuously held *behind* the Japanese lines. The latter dealt with more complex class problems based on the gentry-dominated economy of the populous great plains and valleys reaching to the sea.

The "two fronts" combined in 1949, but the gulf between them was never entirely closed. Liu Shao-ch'i had been chief Politburo commissar in the East China plains and had headed the urban underground. In the post-victory period he became the No. 1 Party bureaucrat supervising organization and training of new cadres. In time, Liu came to personify the urban-oriented Party, with its closer ties with some leading intellectuals more or less influenced by bourgeois Western thought, with those later linked to the Soviet technical aid program, and with part of the working class in turn affected by petit-bourgeois traditions. Mao personified the total indigenous revolutionary experience that was deeply rooted in the vast countryside, with egalitarian traditions realized in the armed forces and their close ties with the peasantry.

The foregoing observations provide no simple "formula" to "explain everything"—no formula could do that—but merely suggest one neglected important facet of a many-prismed complex. It is particularly useful to keep it in mind when seeking to understand the limitations of army dominance in Chinese life today.

There is convincing evidence that Mao Tse-tung had hoped to close the "gap," thoroughly erase the differences noted above, and unite the "two fronts" when he accepted the Party's choice of Liu Shao-ch'i as his first deputy, in 1956, and again when he stepped aside in 1958 to give Liu the responsibility of chief executive. As early as 1959 Mao realized that the gap was widening rather than diminishing, and that Liu was probably a wrong choice. We have seen how events then developed into the cultural revolution of 1966-69.

As far as Liu and the backsliders (as Mao saw them) entrenched in the administrative bureaucracy were concerned, the first aim of the revolution was no mere purge but total destruction of their edifice of state power. The construction stage—the question of "To Whom"[1] to transfer power—was even more difficult. In the first stage, "turned on" by directives in the August, 1966, communiqué, millions of "lower ranks"—cadres, students, workers, non-Party masses—rapidly rose to express long-repressed grievances against some of the Party elite. Branches of the Party and its peripheral organizations—Young Communists, trade unions, Party schools—were seen virtually dissolved by "revolutionary rebels" urged on by Mao's Cultural Revolution Group "at the Center."

New mass organizations—led by Red Guards, workers' congresses, Party rebels—seized local power. Leaders of the "old order" fought back, through surrogate "rebels," to recover control. One provisional committee after another was set up and overthrown; new leaders arose and quickly fell. Under directives from "the Central Group," Shanghai was the first city to form a "three-in-one alliance" —a revolutionary committee consisting of "reliable Party

---

[1] The title of an essay by Mao Tse-tung featured by his partisans during the GPCR.

cadres," representatives of the new mass organizations, and delegates from the army. Very slowly and stormily, other cities and provinces followed.

At many levels the rebels failed to unite on a choice of new forms and leaders; they fell into factions, fought each other, and near-anarchy prevailed. The army, ordered by "the Center" not to use weapons but to "support the left"—meaning true rebels, not puppets of the "old order"—intervened to protect state property. In certain places Red Guards seized arms from the militia and set up command posts, and among them were some persons later defined as counterrevolutionaries. An incipient civil war situation soon prevailed.

The General Political Department of the army was the only experienced *Party* organization which remained intact. By 1967 Mao was obliged to call upon it to end the chaos and, using weapons when necessary, to *"support industry, support agriculture, support the broad masses of the left, establish military control and lead ideological and military training."*

Premier Chou told me that "hundreds of thousands of casualties" were inflicted on the army before and after it began using force to disarm the extremists, end factional fighting, and lead all sectors in the formation of revolutionary committees. Two million "Maoist activists" were drawn from the army to carry out that task. From the revolutionary committees gradually was to be molded a purified and "successor" Party and a reorganized proletarian state.

Thus the army emerged Very Big from the cultural revolution, and looming large in the future. Bigger than the Party? In the last analysis every system, whether feudal, bourgeois, or socialist, depends upon its armed forces for survival. But the army is an instrument of class rule, as Marxists see it, and it cannot be independent of the class interests which support it. "Political power grows out of the barrel of a gun," said Mao, and the army is a "leading component" of the dictatorship of the proletariat; but Mao also said that "the Party commands the gun and the gun must never be allowed to command the Party."

Note that it is the *Party* which commands the army.[2] It also commands the state superstructure, as recent events again demonstrated, and as now frankly acknowledged in the new Party constitution. When issuing directives to the "Party's army" during the cultural revolution Mao acted as Chairman of that Party, which claims identity with the popular interests of the vast majority, the "proletariat." At the Center, the Party should hold command over *all* its components, and the army can be no exception. But when there are divisions in the Party Center those are of course reflected in divisions in the army leadership too.

Acting for and under the Party, the "people's army" of China is a main link with mass life, with which it seeks thoroughly to integrate in organizational, propagandive, production, and service tasks.

The slogan "everyone a soldier"—which goes back to early Party history—is partly fulfilled. All able-bodied adults, male and female, are part of the army through universal service in the militia. What is the use of reserves of several hundred million militia trainees? They familiarize themselves with weapons, tactics, and terrain; they relive revolutionary battles under veterans; they learn leadership principles, relationships between production and defense, unify and "arm themselves with Mao Thought," and come to regard the army as one with the people—rather than a segregated, nonproducing, tax-consuming professional elite. That, at least, is the aim.

"The Party branch is organized on a company basis," said Mao in 1928. "This is an important reason why the Red Army has been able to carry on such arduous fighting without falling apart." Today the population is "on a company basis."

[2] The army will disappear only when, in that Marxist utopia, class war ends and the state "withers away."

Not only the militia but the whole society is "military" in style and organization. From kindergarten up, students work in squads, teams, companies, and brigades. So do workers in factories, institutions, and communes. Every city street has its neighborhood committee, similarly set up. In an auxiliary workshop run by housewives and dependents of workers in a large locomotive plant we visited I heard the middle-aged woman in charge addressed as "commander" by her charges—who were busily washing old rags and mending pants and shoes.

The first duty of this army is "to serve the people." To do so it must propagate and apply the Thought of Mao Tse-tung. Fortunately, that is not *Mein Kampf*. It contains no doctrines of racism, foreign conquest, or armed export of revolution. It does advocate support for social revolutions but not by armed aggression. At home it teaches liberation through the realization of proletarian power—including the "right to rebel" against wrong leadership—and preparedness against war.

To that degree China *is* militarized—and alarming to many who distrust regimentation. *How* the Chinese army is used—"to serve the people"—is what makes it fascinating and unique.

15

"Serving the People"

We are in a school for "deaf and mute" children in Shen-yang, capital of Liaoning province in Northeast China, once called Manchuria by Westerners. The school is run by a P.L.A. medical and propaganda team of five experts in acupuncture. Students arrive here unable to hear or speak but they are not congenitally deaf. They have lost their hearing as a result of measles, meningitis, high fevers of various kinds.

The school nucleus existed before the cultural revolution, we are told by Li Chun-shan, who heads the army team. Students were formerly taught to communicate by sign language. In 1966, when Chairman Mao received millions of rebel Red Guards, this school also sent a squad to Peking, waving the little red books of Mao's Quotations.

"When the students saw Chairman Mao they wept for joy," said Li, "but they could not shout with the others. All they could do was stamp their feet. Seeing this, our commanders told us to pay attention to Chairman Mao's directive, 'Chinese medicine is a great treasure house,' and serve the people. We medical aid workers had already experimented with acupuncture as a cure for deafness. We began more intensive experimentation, on ourselves, pushing the needles beyond the old 'forbidden zone,' as deep as we could stand it.

"In November, 1968, we were sent to take charge of health and acupuncture training in this school. We taught the techniques to the staff and won their support. In a short time many students were able to hear and speak. The first thing they learn to say is 'Long live Chairman Mao!' In two years we have treated 582 students and more than 98 percent have resumed hearing. About 80 percent recite short quotations and can sing, 'The East Is Red.' A fundamental change has occurred. You see no more sign language. Now you hear singing and reading aloud."

Naïve? One must see the captivating faces of the children and hear their high-pitched voices, straining with effort. They range in age from nine to twenty: healthy, warmly clad, eyes glowing, watching P.L.A. commander Li as if he were a god. We see their daily acupuncture treatments: needles inserted deeply behind well-washed ears. "Fear neither hardship nor death!" shouts one lad, close to tears. "Remember 'The Foolish Old Man Who Removed the Mountains'!" calls another.

We visit classrooms where advanced students recite or read aloud. Their work here takes them up to middle-school level. We encourage their efforts with applause. They listen to the foreign "uncle" and "aunt" with ineffably moving smiles of trust and hope. They take our hands in theirs as we walk down the aisles. Then with the help of a nearby middle-school orchestra they put on a performance of songs and dances for us. They follow us to the street, still smiling, clapping hands.

"Wo-men-ti Mei-kuo p'eng-yu, tsai-chien," their shrill farewells echo as we leave them. "Come back, American friends."

Such schools now exist in many Chinese cities and towns. I asked the opinion of a Dutch doctor and his wife, whom I met back in Peking. They had both worked for years in a school for mutes in Amsterdam, using advanced European techniques. They shook their heads. "It's like Lourdes," they said, "faith healing."

Acupuncture may be still unexplained by anatomical theory, but it is much more than Lourdes, as increasing numbers of Western acupuncturists can now attest.

In a commune village in northern Hopei I stop to photograph an attractive stone farmhouse. Going inside, I find it empty except for a comely young woman with needles in her arms and face, and a uniformed young man beside her. She is a barefoot doctor receiving further training in acupuncture from a P.L.A. medical worker. Spread on the wide *k'ang* (a heated-brick sleeping platform) I see large piles of grasses, aromatic herbs, dried tubers, and other ingredients of the Chinese pharmacopoeia. The girl's team has been gathering them from the hills. On the *k'ang* also is her red-cross kit of modern medicines, which includes birth control pills. And this picture is also duplicated in thousands of villages of China.

We spend a night in the home of a peasant family in Sha Shih Yu, "Sandstone Gulch" brigade, not far below the Great Wall. It is a clean, well-built, three-room stone house, with wide exposed beams under a tile roof, and fronted by a neat garden of very green vegetables and a stone-lined private piggery (population two), in a village of similar homes. The mother is a widow with three grown sons under thirty; the two at home are unmarried, so with no dependents their household income is above average. Their rooms hold chests stocked with bedding and clothing, and display a clock, a radio, huge vacuum bottles, electric light bulbs, bicycles, and a large portrait of the Chairman.

No son in the army? The widow, a robust woman with jet-black hair who herself works in the fields, positively blushed at my question. Although healthy and strong, her sons do not have the perfect vision required by army standards. Then she brightens; they are members of the militia, of course. She displays a photograph of one son, now away from home. He is working with the army, a volunteer, she says, on a new dam and power project in the country—"serving the people."

Army teams are used as shock troops to lead in emergencies such as floods and threatened epidemics, to repair or extend irrigation canals, and to lecture schoolchildren. Numerous are the soldier heroes held up for emulation as doers of good deeds. Among them, Lei Feng is the best known. What did he do with his pay? Spend it on himself? No, he saved his money to lend it to people in need. With his leisure? Go fishing? No, he sewed on buttons for his comrades, he tended the sick. He served others. The "Song of Lei Feng" was popular with Red Guards and effective army propaganda before and throughout the cultural revolution.

We spend a morning outside Shenyang with several hundred militia men and women at precision target practice. Mostly under twenty-five, they come from various factories and schools to demonstrate their proficiency at drill and in handling grenades, rifles, machine guns, mortars, antitank guns, against simulated still and moving targets, at ranges up to 300 meters. It's a holiday or sports arena atmosphere: lots of applause, and smiles all around.

The militia, we are told by P.L.A. officers in charge, is divided into: 1) basic "militia with arms," to age twenty-five, whose members stack and maintain weapons where they work; and 2) "ordinary militia," with members from twenty-five to fifty or over, who include reservists and special units. All light weapons are made in the vicinity.

Before a convincing mock-up of a village corner we see an enemy attack. By guerrilla trickery the villagers easily annihilate the invaders. (Applause.) Japanese, Russians, Americans? It is hard to say but foreign devils they certainly are. Next, a family named Hsu marches out: grandfather, aged sixty, his wife, fifty-eight, a son, daughter-in-law, and four grandchildren. The adults work in a locomotive factory. Using submachine guns and rifles, at 100 meters, they demolish their targets in speedy fashion, except for the youngest. Aged eight, wearing a Little Red Soldier uniform, and a bit of a show-off, he takes plenty of time, lying prone, to score three bull's-eyes with an ordinary rifle.

"Hai mei-yu ch'iang kao," says an officer, smiling broadly. "He's not as tall as his rifle."

"You seem to be expecting some unwelcome visitors," I said. "From which direction?"

"We're ready for them, from whatever direction."

The targets were impartially lettered: "Down with American imperialism!" "Down with Soviet social imperialism!" "Down with revisionists of all kinds!"

16

The Army as Builder

Deep in Shensi province, in Northwest China, lies the narrow valley of Nanniwan, about 200 kilometers north of Sian and 90 kilometers southeast of Yenan, headquarters for ten years (1937-47) of the Chinese Communist guerrilla forces, then known as the Eighth Route Army. A good macadam road now connects Yenan to Nanniwan, a few years ago accessible only by two days' journey on foot. The way is through wild canyons, studded with scrub birch, pines, hemlocks, and tamarind, from which our car occasionally flushed a pheasant or gazelle or mountain goat.

"Good hunting," said our guide and host from the Yenan branch of the Sino-Foreign Friendship Association. "Our soldiers who settled Nanniwan had no other meat but wild game when they first came here."

The cultivated valley we reached was narrow but several miles long, enclosed by steep wooded hills. In 1941, when the Yenan base areas were blockaded on the south and west by Nationalist troops and westward and northward by the Japanese, Nanniwan was a pilot project begun in response to Mao's call for self-sufficiency and "ample food and clothing" to be produced by the army's own efforts.

"Any soldier or civilian who likes to eat but does not like to work cannot be considered a good soldier or a good citizen," said Mao. "It is simply wrong to demand grain and money from the masses, as the Kuomintang does, without making every effort to help them to increase production."[1]

To lead the way, the army's 359th Brigade, officered mainly by young veterans of the Long March, broke open the wilderness glen of Nanniwan, each soldier armed with rifle, pick, spade, and enough seed grain to last one season. Like American pioneers, they cleared enough land to plant a crop; they built caves and lean-tos to survive the severe winter, recruited some landless peasants to help them, made wooden hoes and plows, learned to write on birchbark, brought in a first harvest, replanted, cropped enough to sell a surplus for a few farm animals, built wooden spinning machines, made their own woolen cloth, and fought engagements to keep open a smuggling trade with Nationalist territory. After two winters of near-starvation Nanniwan became a self-sufficient forest community.

The story came to us from a man who lived through it: Chu Shao-ch'ing, a lean, windburned hero of the Long March, who was now back in the valley he had helped to clear. Chu had left Nanniwan in 1944, to fight a long string of military engagements. Now, at fifty-three, he was commander of the Fortieth Regiment of the P.L.A. Construction Corps, and Nanniwan was a state farm—"owned by the whole people." In the meeting hall, which was one of a cluster of stout but simply made one-story tile-roofed brick buildings, he briefly explained the evolution of the area.

During the period (1949-52) of land distribution and postrevolutionary consolidation and clean-up of counter-revolutionaries, Nanniwan became a reform-through-labor farm.[2] China does not admit to a category of "political

---

[1] *Selected Works of Mao Tse-tung*, Vol. III (Foreign Languages Press, Peking, 1953), page 133.

[2] See *Red China Today, op. cit.*, pages 352–57.

prisoners"—known here only as "counterrevolutionaries"—
but in practice capital crimes committed with political
motivation are treated more severely than nonpolitical
crimes. As a prison farm, Nanniwan fell under the general
responsibility of Lo Jui-ch'ing, for long head of the
internal security forces, and one of the first top men to
fall during the purge of the cultural revolution.

The reform-through-labor farm apparently was dissolved in 1965, to become a state enterprise where many
ex-convicts remained as settled peasant families. Chu said
that some youths were also recruited locally. Then in the
period 1966-68 "Liu Shao-ch'i's influence here was very
bad. Many of the youths ran away to join the Red Guards
on long travels."

"Could Liu Shao-ch'i have had an influence so far
away—" I broke in.

For what I thought was to be an explanation I was introduced to an old warrior seated next to the commander.
He was vice-chairman of the revolutionary committee of
one of the farm brigades. A man with piercing eyes beneath craggy brows in a leathery face, a couple of teeth
exposed in a frequent grin, he was named Wang Ming-teh.
He looked to be a hundred, but later I noticed him thread-
ing through the fields agile as a youth. He was sixty-six,
he told us. It turned out that Wang and Chu had joined
the same regiment in the old Red Army in Hunan, on the
same day, in 1933, in the same *squad*, and had remained
together practically ever since.

Wang had fought a hundred battles and in his wandering discourse seemed prepared to describe each, being
especially eloquent when "recalling past bitterness" about
Nanniwan. He reminded me of the Californian in John
Steinbeck's story, "The Leader of the People," who had
led a wagon train across the Rockies and could never be
stopped on that subject once he was launched.

Time waxed on during Wang's interminable, fascinating
reminiscences; one story about how wild grasses were
made to produce a "beautiful dye" for the homespun

wool of the pioneer days took a semester or two to relate and somewhere we lost my question about Liu Shao-ch'i, so that I never learned how he had influenced the situation in this remote spot.

After the "bad years," 1966-67, the army had taken over the farm and by now, 1970, production was much improved. Targets were set which would soon bring Nanniwan abreast of the high yields of most state farms, generally far above the commune-collective average.

According to Commander Chu, Nanniwan farm now had a total of 18,000 hectares of grain, fruit, and forest lands. About 30,000 people were under his command, with a mixed working force of peasant families long settled here (including some ex-landlords and ex-convicts), Party cadres, students, and former Red Guards, backed by a regiment of soldier-worker-peasant labor.

Total farm output here belonged to the state. Operations were based on a wage system, as in other state enterprises. Shelter was provided free and the average wage was 40 yuan per month, which is a bit less than the average factory wage for semiskilled labor but higher than the cash income of a farm commune member. At Nanniwan the worker must, however, pay for his own food at an average cost of 12 yuan a month. Settled peasant families who owned their own homes, kitchens, and private plots were paid less in cash, on a work-point basis.

The most interesting corner of Nanniwan was its May Seventh Cadres' School for the reeducation of high Party functionaries, which I shall describe after noting a few other army operations of a kind not to be seen every day.

Many state-owned farms, maybe all on the frontiers, have long been under some kind of army supervision, but that increased greatly during the cultural revolution. One state farm I had previously visited, at Kiamusze (Chiamusu), not far from Siberia, was 90 percent mechanized and really a factory farm, operating on a straight-wage basis. In agricultural communes mechanization is less than 15 percent and ownership and accounting rest with the villagers in theory, and to an important extent in practice. The last official figure[3] available for the area of state farms was ten million acres, or about 4 percent of the total cultivated land. Today it may be 50 percent higher.

State farms supervised by the P.L.A. and its Party leadership existed in every province and on every frontier. Wherever May Seventh schools opened new land, that also became "owned by the whole people." Along the seacoast and on inland waterways the Army Construction Corps was busy reclaiming marginal land to put to state agricultural use.

From Turkestan to the frosty Siberian frontier the army was building and settling new communities integrated with the defense system. One of the difficulties of disengaging Chinese and Russian armed forces along their 5,000-mile frontier was said to be that in many areas the Chinese side was densely inhabited, whereas long stretches of the Russian Siberian and Mongolian frontier were sparsely peopled except for troops. For the Russians, to keep a million border troops supplied, without much local production support, was a far more expensive operation than that of the more or less self-sufficient Chinese forces integrated with state farms. If the armed forces on both sides withdrew 10 kilometers in some places that would leave an empty view on the Russian side but multitudes of settlers (and militiamen?) on the Chinese side. That prospect disturbed the Soviet authorities.

Who provided the settlers, the labor, apart from the fighting forces themselves? Party cadres formed a small percentage of it. Under the new educational system middle-school graduates spent three years at manual labor before they went on to higher education, *if* they were

---

[3] Given to me in an interview with Wu Chen, Vice-Minister of Agriculture, December 12, 1964.

selected by their squads and companies. Their schools decided, within plans set by regional revolutionary committees, how many students to assign to the universities, armed forces, factories, farms, or frontiers. Such youths had apprentice status and were provided only with food, clothing, and a few yuan of "pocket money." The Army Construction Corps trained hundreds of thousands—no foreigner knew how many—and joined them with skilled and unskilled labor drawn from the cities. Many settled down permanently at the site of their building work.

The army engaged in large afforestation and housing projects and built strategic dams, power plants, bridges, tunnels, and roads. It had an important role in pollution control. During the cultural revolution the P.L.A. Construction Corps completed the difficult Chengtu-Kunming railway which now connects Vietnam with Turkestan. In Peking it built the new subway. In all China it supervised the communications network. The extensive air-raid shelter system was constructed under army direction. Naval officers were in command of the Shanghai ship-building yards when I visited new ocean liners being launched there. In rural communes the army was represented through the militia down to the brigade and production team level. And the P.L.A. of course operated all military and nuclear industries.

In organized cultural life army officers played leading roles in managing revolutionary committees. In these "three-way alliances" ("reliable Party cadres," mass organization delegates, and "responsible military representatives"), the "responsibles" were always in a minority and nearly always I found them commanding the chair. Not only universities and hospitals were under ideological indoctrination by the P.L.A. General Political Department. So was the revolutionary committee of a ballet company we visited backstage in Sian, as was another in Shanghai.

One place I did not see a uniformed man in the director's chair was the May Seventh School at Nanniwan.

17

Alice in Nanniwan

Writing about May Seventh schools away from China
makes one feel that it all must have happened behind the
looking glass. There on the spot it seemed plausible and
even a good thing, but to explain to outsiders? One recalls
the Red Queen's advice to Alice, "Curtsey while you're
thinking what to say. It saves time." Better still, "Begin
at the beginning, and go on till you come to the end: then
stop."

In one sense it seems too good to be true: May Seventh
schools are reform schools for reformers. In Nanniwan's
old reform-through-labor farm days the inmates were in-
voluntary residents: recalcitrant landlords, counterrevolutionaries, and ordinary criminals working out their time
while studying the texts of socialism, to transform themselves into good citizens of an inchoate proletarian state.
At the Nanniwan May Seventh Cadres' School, typical of
many, there were Party functionaries who had committed
themselves, or been committed by their groups, to relearn
the meaning of meaning—socialist meaning. They had
become "divorced from production and reality," and now
sought to "integrate themselves with the masses" and
"learn from the peasants and workers."

In China, as everywhere else, everything that happens
is logical and explainable if we can see it in the context of

historical problems which condition the political means of their solution. "Freedom is the recognition of necessity," says Mao, echoing Marx. If so, May Seventh schools are no exception.

They began in fulfillment of a directive issued by Chairman Mao on May 7, 1968: "Going down to do manual labor gives vast numbers of cadres an excellent opportunity to study once again; and this should be done by all cadres except those who are old, weak, ill, or disabled." Early that year the revolutionary committees formed as organs of power during the cultural revolution, and led by the Army-in-the-Party, began to promote treks of "vast numbers of cadres" to the countryside to "do manual labor." Some of them were administrative heads of great institutions—universities, factories, rural and urban governing councils—and some were Party schoolteachers or strictly organizational bosses.

Why a university president, for example?

The whole intellectual life of the country, it was said, had been slipping back into an old pattern dominated by the traditional maxim of Mencius: "He who uses his mind rules; he who labors with his hands is ruled." (You can't make a silk purse from a sow's ear.) Bourgeois-trained directors of middle schools and universities were weeding out the peasant-born, worker-born students—those with an inferior start—by tougher and tougher examinations. Instead of becoming shorter and more practically related to mass needs, courses were being extended to six and eight or more years in many university specialties.

"Yet the social consequences of this were hardly encouraging to anyone who wished to build a radically new social order, for as Mao saw it, the universities were contributing to social stratification and were training an elite motivated by selfish ambition," wrote an American scholar, John Gardner, in his contribution, "Educated Youth and Urban-Rural Inequalities," to a carefully researched 1971 symposium on China.

One of the major consequences of the reemphasis on professionalism was a reduction in the number of university students from worker and peasant families, and a corresponding increase in those from the families of senior cadres and the "exploiting classes" . . . Thus at Peking University the number of students from worker and peasant families fell from nearly 67 percent in 1958 to only 38 percent in 1962, while the number of students of "exploiting class" background more than doubled. Many of the university's professors were contemptuous of proletarian students, referring to them as "coarse teacups not amenable to fancy carving" and resenting the fact that such students had obtained university places by means of [political] "ladders." Of 237 students admitted to the eight departments of natural science in 1958 only 45 graduated with their original class, the others having been expelled or held back . . .

At Peking Technical College more than 800 of the 919 cadres and military men sent there as students were "weeded out," as were 200 at Tsinghua. Of 108 students expelled from Peking Commercial College, some 94 percent were of working class origin . . . Han Suyin, a well-informed and favored visitor to China, has written [1967]: "Investigations into the universities and senior middle schools in the cities provided a shock; after seventeen years of socialist China, over 40 percent of the students were still from bourgeois, landlord, and capitalist families, even if these were only 5 percent of the population."[1]

The revolution in education is in itself a vastly important subject, but some glimpse of its relevance is here indispensable in order to explain May Seventh schools. Nanniwan's school body included some teachers and was made up mainly of seasoned Party executives who also were responsible for education in one way or another.

[1] John Wilson Lewis, editor, *The City in Communist China* (Palo Alto, Calif., 1971), pages 266–67.

Liu Yu-sheng introduced himself as vice-chairman of the management committee. He was tall, erect, thirtyish, tanned and muscular. Otherwise he was a type recognizable as "intellectual"—which years ago often meant merely literate but now implies at least a middle-school background. Liu had been with the school from its inception on October 4 two years earlier. It had begun with 467 persons drawn from eleven organizations in greater Sian, capital of Shensi province.

They did not call themselves students; they were "May 7 fighters," Mr. Liu explained.

"Our main task is to train senior leaders of the Sian municipal and adjacent county level. Our fundamental principles are: to act in accordance with the Thought of Mao Tse-tung; to remold our world outlook; to let cadres learn from the workers and peasants and integrate with them in a fundamental way; to do mass work while studying and to do manual work while criticizing the bourgeois outlook.

"The old Party schools were divorced from labor, from the masses, from production and reality. Our school also differs from the old state farms, which went in only for production. Now after two years of tempering we have supplied 414 revolutionary cadres. Some of them have gone back to the city but many have settled down in the countryside. Any questions?"

Who was Mr. Liu? A graduate of the school himself, he had stayed on as political leader. What was he doing before? A "leader of youth work in the city"—likely meaning the secretariat of the Young Communist League. Beside him sat a rather pretty young woman, Hsu Chiu-feng, who had been Party chairman of the East Section Tung Fang Hung (East Is Red) commune of Sian. Now she was in the school's "first company of rice planters." She also seemed in charge of the kitchen, from which presently poured (half of the dozen people at the table helping) a series of platters heaped with fresh pork, corn on the cob, baked sweet potatoes, squash, milk, scrambled eggs, apples, and a dozen other delicious products of the school farm.

They had 920 *mou* (153 acres),[2] 53 cows, more than 300 pigs, and umpteen ducks and chickens. Eight hundred *mou* were in rice and other grain; output 170,000 catties (85 tons) last year. Forty *mou* were in vegetables and fruit, 50 in potatoes, 30 in hemp. They now numbered 216 able-bodied "May 7 fighters," about a fourth of them women, average age thirty to forty, with a sprinkling of older people, up to age sixty-one. They included *seven* doctors. The farm now seemed about self-sufficient in food, shelter, and fuel—they had built a small dam and power plant—but living was on a primitive level.

The "fighters" had opened some new land; they built houses (and furniture) from hand-hewn timbers, did all the labor chores—with the advice of peasants borrowed from the state farm—and in slack time studied and debated politics, under army leaders. In six months or a year they might achieve "Mao activism." What was an activist? A person *whose squad voted him to be* one who was not just a good student but one who "applied the Thought of Mao Tse-tung in a living way."

While at the school, I was told, all members retained the wage status they had had according to their rank in the cadre system, their families at home maintaining themselves as formerly.

Thirty people were in the management committee, and the heads of various departments submitted themselves to interviewing while we consumed their modest banquet. And how delightful it was, too, to eat fresh, simple food, far from the gourmet hotel fare, with the reformed reformers who had produced it!

There was T'an Chung, for example, aged forty-eight, who wore a mauve jacket and had a relaxed smile exposing

[2] A *mou* is about one-sixth of an acre.

fine white teeth. Formerly a senior cadre member of the Sian revolutionary committee, he was now in charge of the school pigsties and had just been chosen an activist "by the fighters in our company." He quoted Mao about "going down to the countryside" and said he had seized the "opportunity."

"Actually I don't consider myself very good at Mao. I was in a leading position but divorced from reality, so I chose to come here. They put me to work in the pigsty, shoveling shit, and learning to breed pigs. I studied Chairman Mao—'fear neither hardship nor death'—and integrated with the peasants, who were my good teachers. It's very interesting work. Gradually I'm getting closer to the masses and remolding my world outlook." The last phrase meant "fighting myself" and becoming a prole-tarian in outlook.

Take Li Wan-chun, in his fifties, formerly in the secre-tariat of the Sian Party Committee. He had a long revolutionary history going back to Yenan days, but—spoiled by "sugar bullets" of the city—he lost touch with the countryside. Now he was "planting corn and rice," studying Mao Tse-tung Thought and other Marxist liter-ature—but still had "a long way to go."

Liu Wen-yuan, fortyish, had joined the Party in 1950, graduated from university in 1960, and risen to be dean of the Twenty-fourth Middle School of Sian. He had never really known how hard peasants work. How could he teach? Now he was a *wu-ch'i chan-shih*—a May 7 fighter —"doing manual labor in the grain fields." He was still in the "struggle" (to free himself from a bad class back-ground) and "self-criticism" stage, with hopes of "trans-formation" into a comrade' with a "new world outlook."

Next to him sat Wang Yi-p'ing, thirty-eight, ex-secretary of the Sian Young Communist League—now being recon-stituted. A Yenan student in 1948, he had fallen into evil ways in the city, seduced by easy-living Party priv-ileges under the revisionists. He had forgotten hardship.

He had become a bureaucrat, and "bureaucrats and the workers and middle-poor peasants are acutely *antagonistic classes*," said Mao. The bureaucrats were "becoming capitalist vampires to the workers. How can they have sufficient understanding?" Now in his second year in the school, Wang was not yet an activist, but already "leader of the school's No. 1 rice-planting company." That was progress.

"At the beginning," said Liu the director, "we had many 'twists and turns,' 'undergoing struggle.' Why set up a forest school 800 *li* [240 miles] from Sian? Some students were 'afraid of hardship.' To toughen them we made it a tradition for each arrival to march the 180 *li* from here to Yenan and back. We invited veterans of the 359th Brigade to come to lecture us on 'past bitterness' here. Gradually we have developed deep proletarian feelings toward Chairman Mao and now see the wisdom of Nanniwan as a school site.

"Here we have relived revolutionary conditions. Things were very poor at first: broken-down caves and a few buildings, overgrown or uncleared fields, few tools. Should we have asked for help from Sian? The majority said no. We followed the 359th Brigade tradition of self-reliance. Made beds and furniture from trees, made houses the same way, made tools and baskets, learned to make tiles.

"We built our own generator—we did get a loan for that. Last spring we had a deluge that covered the spillway with four inches of mud and ravaged our rice fields. 'The Foolish Old Man Who Removed the Mountains' came to our rescue. In his spirit we cleared the spillway, carried 500 cubic meters of earth by hand, and restored our rice fields in time to replant and get a good crop. Self-reliance changed our mental outlook. 'With two hands you can do anything' became our slogan."

So it went. We devoted the afternoon to a tour of the fields, meeting more "fighters" and their peasant comrades, viewing the well-kept fields and stout new buildings, and ending up with a close inspection of the piggeries, neatly constructed in hillside caves. Here were good people seemingly satisfied in doing humble work almost as well as the peasants. At the time I was impressed by their admirable spirit and even envious of the benefits of their strong group therapy. Only now, reflecting on my notes in bourgeois surroundings, do I remember the White Queen. "I can't believe *that!*" said Alice. "Can't you?" said the Queen in a pitying tone. "I daresay you haven't had much practice. When I was your age, I always did it for half-an-hour a day. Why, sometimes I've believed as many as six impossible things before breakfast."

Millions of people have been through May Seventh schools. It is said that in the future all Party members will do so. My interpreter, Yao Wei, had spent a year working in such a commune school. His wife, a Russian-language specialist, was still in one. My old friend Huang Hua, now China's Permanent Representative to the United Nations, had been through such a "tempering" in 1969, as had his wife, also a Party leader. Recalled from their overseas posts, all Chinese diplomats had worked in commune schools or equivalents.

Artists too? "Let us drive opera singers, poets, playwrights, and men of letters out of the cities," Mao was reported as saying, "and drive all of them to the countryside. Send them down to villages and factories in groups and at different times. Do not let them stay in offices all the time; they cannot write anything there."[3] And they went, too, and many were still being "tempered" there when I looked for them in the cities.

Are all these people sincerely "reformed"? Certainly not all. Far fewer would be converted if they were simply "sent down" by *force majeure*. The system works more subtly than that, as explained to me by an old friend who had himself done his season in the sun.

[3] Jerome Ch'en, *Mao Papers, op. cit.*, page 95.

"It's like this. In whatever work you are normally doing you belong to a squad, part of a company. Two hours a day, two or three times a week, you have study sessions, and once a week or so you meet jointly with other squads. You don't just sit and memorize Mao. You take a piece of his work for a theme, you read it aloud, and then you discuss what it means in practical application. Based on that, there is criticism and self-criticism about how far from reality you are in your daily work. Sometimes it gets very hot, so deflates the ego, so bares the soul, a man feels he needs a purge. That's when he volunteers to go down to the countryside."

Like getting religion? Hitting the sawdust trail?

"What if the feeling never reaches certain persons?"

"Well, it may not, but after a while everyone has gone but you, hints are dropped, you begin to feel eyes are on you, it's your turn—and you know they're trying to *help* you. In some cases the whole squad or group may apply for permission to go down together. It's good for every-body to get away from routine—to know what labor is. Yes, we all come back better for the experience."

If you are young it's easier and it can be fun. If you are older and a professional person it can seem a dreadful waste of the little time that is left. If you are not used to manual toil it can be very tough, especially if the squad leadership is "bad." I knew people who had spent months bending over and kneeling in rice fields, hauling heavy loads, doing tasks beyond their physical ability, who suffered severely. More often it is mental suffering, for intellectuals—and among intellectuals of the world none has traditionally been more arrogant in disdaining hand labor than the Chinese—who find it inwardly impossible to equalize themselves with a peasant or soldier scarcely able to read and write.

Combining labor with brain work was so novel to most Chinese intellectuals that news that the practice existed even in American bourgeois society—though nowadays less frequently so—was one of those "impossible things" to believe. Before I was twenty-three I had worked as a printer's devil, waiter, farm hand, and other odd tasks during school vacations or after school hours, and had later taken pride in work as a seaman. In that way I learned to respect labor and despise idleness. But such work would not attract me now, and I realize that working to make money or get experience is not the same as doing it for political reasons; and certainly I had not sought to "equalize myself" with peasant or laborer. To that extent the spiritual content was lacking—as it is glaringly so now in labor philosophy in all capitalist societies.

Before leaving this subject it should be noted that serious cases of "revisionists" up to and including those named as counterrevolutionaries in China received far more severe treatment than volunteering to become "May 7 fighters." According to Red Guard claims, some Kuomintang spies and professional saboteurs were uncovered. Although Mao Tse-tung stressed again and again that even "enemies of the people" were never to be beaten or physically abused, his words went unheeded in thousands of instances. Many were those arrested by Red Guard vigilantes in the early days of the cultural revolution on trumped-up charges. Once in custody, the whole political and family background of the victim had to be investigated. As power committees rose and fell, people arrested by one group might be liberated by another, only to seek revenge by accusing their accusers. By the time the army intervened and swept aside the factions, tens of thousands of case histories once again had to be reviewed. In all these transitions there were always those who had abused their temporary power to beat or drive to "suicide" their chosen victims—sometimes important and useful revolutionaries who had at most made "a few mistakes" in their zeal to follow the rules of "self-cultivation."

There were two things about the Great Proletarian Cultural Revolution, Mao Tse-tung said to me, of which he disapproved. One was lying. (Open warfare was better than verbal deceit.) . . .

The second thing the Chairman was most unhappy about was the maltreatment of "captives." (Arrested persons.) That was not the way of the Red Army or the People's Liberation Army during past wars. . . .

"What I tell you three times," to move back to Lewis Carroll once more, "is *true*." But nobody knew better than Chairman Mao that though he might say it three thousand times there would always be deaf men among those who claimed power in his name. And who was it, after all, who said, "Revolution is not a dinner party . . ."?

18

The Army and the People

Men in uniform are omnipresent in China, but most of them go unarmed among the people, their public behavior is exemplary, and any visitor can quickly see that the armed forces are popular. Public schools are filled with Little Red Soldiers; nearly every family I met aspired to have at least one son or daughter able to satisfy the high P.L.A. entrance requirements. The state constitution lists service in the armed forces as one of the citizen's "rights and duties." Among soldiers I questioned in barracks and elsewhere I never met one who could conceive of being a "conscientious objector"—once the term was explained to him—or imagine himself engaged in a future war in which his country might be "wrong."[1]

It is a highly disciplined, democratic, worker-peasant army and now at the height of its prestige, enjoying a major role of leadership in the many directions I have indicated. It is unquestionably less burdensome to the population than most armies. It is self-policing. It grows much of the food it consumes, has no camp followers, and is ever ready to help in emergencies in field or factory.

Since 1959, the P.L.A. had almost recovered the "working style" of the Yenan days. Symbols of rank—epaulettes,

[1] See *Red China Today, op. cit.*, page 287.

tailored uniforms, hard hats, medals—and other overt signs
of an officer caste, copied from the Russian army, disappeared in the early sixties. Exchanges of criticism between
officers and men, and periodic service in the ranks for
officers, were restored. All combat officers rose from the
ranks. Differences in pay and living conditions had been
reduced as between officers and men, although they were
still far from being as "equal" as in the Yenan armies.

Training places great stress on politics, and politics
means relations with the people. Among rules to be memorized (and *sung*) are Eight Points for Attention, still
essentially the same as in the original Red Army: Speak
politely; pay fairly for what you buy; return everything
you borrow from the people; pay for anything you damage; don't hit or swear at people; don't damage crops;
don't take liberties with women; and don't mistreat captives. In addition, there are the "three main rules of
discipline": Obey orders in all your actions; don't take a
single needle or piece of thread from the masses; and turn
in everything captured.

There is also something called the "three-eight working
style," expressed in Chinese in three phrases plus eight
characters. The three phrases are: a firm and correct
political orientation; a plain, hard-working style; and
flexibility in strategy and tactics. The eight characters
call for unity, alertness, earnestness, and liveliness. Individuals or companies receive certificates of merit for being
"four goods," meaning those who are good in the "three-
eight working style," in political and ideological work,
military training, and in their everyday behavior.

Anybody with a "four-goods" award in the family
proudly frames it for display beside a portrait of Chairman Mao.

In general, the theory of military training is that it
must be subordinated to ideological excellence, in accordance with Mao's dictum, "Politics in command." The
guideline is the "four firsts": as between man and weapon,

give first place to man; as between political and other work, give first place to political work; as between ideological and routine tasks in political work, give first place to ideological work; and in ideological work, as between ideas in books and living ideas currently in people's minds, give first place to the latter.

Those basic principles reflect Mao's belief that "man is more important than weapons," and that without primacy for the moral-political factor, superior weapons or numbers count for little. Such concepts in turn reflect Mao's early assimilation of the teachings of Sun Tzu (circa 350-450 B.C.), master strategist of ancient China, whose *Art of War* is full of wisdom as bright as new coinage. Sun Tzu said that in strategy there are five fundamental factors, and the "first of these factors is moral influence . . . that which causes the people to be in harmony with their leaders, so that they will accompany them in life and unto death without fear of mortal peril."[2]

"Politics in command" does not mean, of course, that the P.L.A. slights modern weapons and their expert use. "Politics and technology must be unified," said Mao. "This is the meaning of Red *and* expert." No attempt can be made here to compete with Western intelligence agencies in estimating China's weaponry except in a general sense. It is hardly questioned that the P.L.A.'s 3,000,-000-man regular army possesses the most formidable land forces in Asia, backed by millions of trained reserves and auxiliaries. Its infantry and artillery weapons have been used very effectively in Vietnam, as have its antiaircraft guns. The P.L.A. is self-sufficient in all such weapons and in modern armor. Since the early sixties China has made jet engines for her output of copies of the Soviet MIG-19, and by 1970 was reported to have in production new jet aircraft of her own design said to be superior to the Rus-

---

[2] Sun Tzu, *The Art of War*, translated by Samuel Griffith (New York, 1963), pages 63–64.

sian MIG-21. She was also producing light and medium jet bombers in limited quantities.

Outclassed as China is by the superpowers in the air and in surface and submarine naval vessels, she neverthe-less has a combined-arms capability adequate to deter any invader who might seek by conventional weapons to test her great defensive power. The latter had by 1971 come to include a small but sobering nuclear arsenal and means of regional delivery sufficient greatly to reduce a former sense of helplessness before atomic threats. Already no power could atomize China without suffering severe reprisals. China's early potential for interconti-nental bomb messages was a major factor in the Nixon Administration's decision to accept the People's Republic as a reality and seek a new relationship between states in some rational system of peaceful coexistence.

I believe all that is understood by most of "the people," including bright old peasants whom I have heard exult in their pride as participants in China's self-reliant rise to strength after more than a century of humiliation and near-destruction by Western and Japanese invaders. For them the arms of China are a collective achievement—bought very dearly by their toil—and one which propaganda-education teaches them to accept as "their own." Do they all believe it? Mao himself conceded that "5 percent" were still "opposed to socialism." For that 5 percent— more or less?—is the army an oppressor dividing them from recovery of their ancestral lands? or from "becoming rich and high officials"? or perhaps Taoist monks? or fancy-free artists? or writers of books "divorced from reality"? Most of the several hundreds who manage to flee to Hongkong every month seem to be tempted by dreams of making that plain old manure known as money. Rarely indeed is a P.L.A. veteran found among them.

"The army is a big school," Mao has kept repeating, where soldiers learn to despise individual acquisitiveness. They should "learn politics, military affairs, and culture, and engage in agricultural production. [The army] can build up its own middle- and small-size workshops to produce goods for its own use and the exchange of other goods of equal value . . . In this way, it carries out military-educational, military-agricultural, military-industrial, and military-civilian work . . . [so that] the tremendous power of several million soldiers will be felt."[3]

The old Chinese adage was "Do not use good iron to make nails or good men to make soldiers." In Kuomintang China I used to see illiterate conscripts dragged in with ropes around their necks. Officers commonly squeezed pay and rations, beat men if they complained, and themselves engaged in business and black-market operations, taking care of their personal political careers and families first, their soldiers last. (Somewhat as among some ARVN officers in South Vietnam.) Today's P.L.A. "fighter" is literate, reads Mao about what a good commander should be, knows his rights, and may complain at "struggle" and "criticism" meetings. Cases of corrupt officers are not unheard of, but they are perhaps even rarer than premarital sex.

This "quality" army costs the people unbelievably little as far as base pay and maintenance are concerned. How much is that?

In October, 1970, I sat at dinner next to Nieh Jungchen, whom I first met in 1936, who later became a marshal and now was head of the Nuclear Sciences Development Commission. I learned no bomb secrets but he talked at length about the P.L.A. Each soldier was issued three shirts a year, winter and summer or mountain shoes, complete winter and summer uniforms, and unlimited food rations. Recruits are not accepted, as a rule, if needed for support of their parents; in special cases allowances are made for family support. The average recruit, unmarried, received training, education, medical care, and entertainment free and had no food, shelter, or other living expenses. His base pay of 6 yuan

[3] Jerome Ch'en, *Mao Papers, op. cit.*, page 104.

per month was therefore considered ample pocket money by Nieh Jung-chen.

Later, in Chekiang, I met General Chou Wen-chiang, who told me that service pay had been raised to 12 to 15 yuan a month for the equivalent of a pfc. It was also General Chou who told me that majority officers had recently taken a voluntary cut of 30 percent. That might bring a full general's income down to about 350 yuan a month, according to wage scales given to me in the sixties.[4] (Officers used to get 5 yuan a month in the Red Army when I first met Nieh Jung-chen.) A lieutenant colonel in an army propaganda team told me his monthly pay was 70 yuan—a reduction of about 40 percent. Otherwise, the cultural revolution had brought no wage leveling to the P.L.A.; middle officers' pay remained unchanged while lower ranks had risen and top ranks deflated.

Like civilian organizations, the army followed the socialist rule, "From each according to his ability, to each according to the work performed"—with age, years of service, family responsibilities, and rank taken into account. Majority officers and higher still received many side benefits, including special quarters and the use of cars.

All that may read well, but was there not still a certain uneasiness in China about the power role inherited by the army following the breakup of the top Party bureaucracy? A peasant family used to aspire to put one son through school in the hope that he could then become rich and powerful. "Becoming a cadre in order to become a high official" was an inherited mental state constantly condemned and one reason given for May Seventh schools. What about "becoming a soldier in order to become a high officer"?

One was reminded that army cadres were after all less than one-tenth of the former Party membership. Could

[4] See *Red China Today, op. cit.*, page 285.

they run the vast country—plus all their production and defense tasks—alone? But were not the old "top Party persons taking the capitalist road" called a "handful"? What would prevent a Party military elite from succeeding to the power of the old bureaucratic elite?

I have already quoted, in part, the answer given by the man with the heaviest responsibilities in reconstructing the dismantled state and Party superstructure from 1967 onward. The most experienced top-ranking state builder left in office after the assault on the Liu Shao-ch'i power structure, Premier Chou En-lai continued to enjoy wide confidence among all three elements of those revolutionary committees which somehow had to be welded into united administrative teams. That involved the delicate job of "liberating" technicians and other experienced Party cadres put through the wringer by the army-completed purge. Many of them preferred to remain in obscurity or avoid new responsibilities. An equally hard task was to inject into those teams enough "new blood," drawn from the ranks of the workers' congresses (which replaced the labor unions) and from the peasant communes, to make the body politic more directly answerable to the masses—the non-Party, nonarmy majority.

An army elite? An army bureaucratic Establishment? "In our socialist state," Chou En-lai replied, "we are all equal within the Party, whether you work in the government, in the Party, or in the army. Once army cadres go to work in government organs they become government workers and are no longer in charge of army work. They are in fact transferred from the army. So in a few years they become just like us."

"Just like us"—meaning like Chou En-lai? Fifty years of revolutionary experience produced, in Chou, a man for all seasons. Could the new mixture produce proletarian successors fast enough to take over before the elders left? I thought of this as I did more "going down to the countryside" myself.

Part Five

People's Communes

19

Beginnings

"Agriculture is the foundation and industry is the leading factor" has been the guiding principle of Chinese economic practice since 1960. At that time of near-famine and general crisis China's leaders abandoned overemphasis on heavy industry and underinvestment in agriculture. Without Soviet aid, China could not do otherwise than adopt the slogan "self-reliance." Setting aside borrowed Soviet paradigms, they "let industry serve agriculture," and aimed to develop the hinterland by their own efforts alone, in a better balance between town and countryside.

Above all, Mao sought to change the environment of Chinese man—and thereby to change man himself. The place modernization had to occur most dramatically was the rural areas, homeland of the vast majority.

By 1971 agricultural communes covered 95 percent of the cultivable land. All of it was collective property except for 5 to 7 percent still held in garden plots privately owned by the peasants. Not much more than 5 percent was in nationalized or state farm enterprises "owned by the whole people."

China is of continental proportions—about the size of Europe and occidental Russia combined—but two-thirds of it is steeply mountainous or wasteland or desert. Reclamation still largely depended on hand labor and the entire planted area was only some 13 percent of the total surface. Cultivated and thickly populated regions still lay mostly in the eastern half of China. In densely crowded deltas the available land was less than 700 square meters per person, but double and triple cropping had become common, helped by greater use of organic and chemical fertilizer—both local products—as had irrigation, hybrid seeds, and other improved farming methods.

China's 1,800 counties were divided into about 70,000 farm communes, according to Premier Chou, which were in turn subdivided into 750,000 production teams or villages. A brigade may hold several or more production teams, which are the basic collective land ownership and accounting units. Brigades own the heavier tools and small industry. They correspond in size to a *hsiang* or district. The communes group together a number of brigades and are administrative subunits of the county.

In the communes about 550,000,000 people must feed themselves and the cities and county towns, produce a surplus from some 100 million hectares planted in grain, and from 20 million hectares devoted to cotton, tea, edible oils, tobacco, ramie, sericulture, and livestock and other "cash crops"—sufficient to bring a profit to themselves and government purchasing monopolies, *and* accumulate capital savings to finance their own modernization, with minimal help from the state.

On the steady growth of wealth under intelligent management and zealous labor of the communes depends the whole future and success or failure of socialism in China.

During three visits to the People's Republic since 1960 I have seen more than thirty communes, from the far north, near the Siberian frontier, to Yunnan, above Vietnam. This time I saw something of eleven communes, including three I had known in 1960, which I asked to revisit. The revisits revealed improvements in cultivating methods, irrigation works, electrification, mechanization, land reclamation, housing, and small industries—much more than in higher cash incomes. After eight years of agricultural growth most peasants now believe in the reality of the "five guarantees" (promised by Party directives) to people too old to work: adequate food, shelter and clothing, fuel, medical care, and proper burial (cremation).

"Adequate"? China's communes are still very poor by material standards of Western landowning farmers. The livelihood they provide is "adequate," however, beyond the former dreams of the landless and perennially overworked, hungry illiterates who were most of the peasants in prerevolutionary China.

20

Sentimental Journey

The poorest commune brigade I saw in 1970 was in Pao
An (now called Tze Dan), deep in central Shensi province, in Northwest China. There the average *gross*
income per household was the equivalent of less than $80
a year. (That was more than double the sum a decade
ago.) By contrast, a "rich" suburban commune was Horse
Bridge, with a population of 36,000 and about an hour's
drive from Shanghai. In a mixed grain- and cotton-
growing area, annual gross output value in 1970 at Horse
Bridge was about $720 per household.

Out of the brigade's gross income, state taxes take 3 to
8 percent, included in operating expenses of about 40 to
50 percent. From 15 to 20 percent of the grain is ear-
marked for quotas delivered to the state at fixed prices.
Net income includes industrial output, livestock, and
"cash crops." From 10 to 25 percent or more is set aside
for the public accumulation fund for investment in equip-
ment and improvements, welfare and loan funds, medical
insurance, and old-age care. Of this amount 80 to 85
percent is retained by the brigade while the balance goes
to commune investment and overhead.

The net income at Horse Bridge in 1969 was about
$102 per worker-member and the average household
(4.6) unit netted about $274. In a nonmechanized Pao

An brigade, where taxes apparently took only about 3 percent of the gross, the net household income seemed to be one-third that of semimechanized Horse Bridge. In the latter, commune and brigade industries—boat building, construction materials, machinery, electric transformers, etc.—accounted for more than 25 percent of combined output value. That is exceptionally high, and a still distant national goal, but many communes now own machine-making, mini-tractor, cement, and small fertilizer plants which meet their own needs on the road to modernization.

Converting yuan into dollars, as I have done here—at the official exchange rate of 2.40 yuan to the dollar—can be quite misleading. In Chinese farm commodity economy the peasants are paid mostly in grain. They sell their surplus, over and above their personal needs—from one-quarter to one-half their share—at state market prices. Their cash income in yuan has a much greater purchasing value than the nominal exchange equivalent abroad, as I have shown in prices quoted earlier.

Many communes now breed their own fish in newly made reservoirs and canals, and part of the catch is in "free distribution" to member families. Vegetables are either home grown or so cheap as to be minor budget items. "Private pigs" (bred on family-owned plots) now add from $10 to as much as $60 a year to many household incomes. The family may prefer to eat pork frequently and get less cash income. (In former times the average peasant tasted meat only two or three times a year.) Commune families own their homes and have no rent to pay, but they cannot sell or rent to others. And the greatest sector of the commune's wealth is nonliquidatable—the member's share in collective capital investments of savings in farm improvements and land ownership.

Wages or shares in the collective income are now decided by the individual's estimate of value of his own work points—an honor system—which is then accepted or reduced or raised in judgments made by his own work team. As overclaims denied by one's neighbors mean a loss of face the tendency is understatement. Work teams choose their own leaders, production teams likewise, and the brigade leadership now consists of a revolutionary committee the majority of whom are farm workers, able to keep party cadres from making arbitrary decisions, as they often did before the cultural revolution. At brigade and production-team levels management and allocation of funds are semiautonomous within lines set by overall commune and state planning. Women theoretically have equal voice in proportion to their labor contribution, which is not much less than that of men, but in practice they are still much underrepresented.

Benefits commune life has brought to the peasant are not all to be measured by a full belly, bodily warmth, better dwellings, good bedding, vacuum bottles, bicycles, or a bit of cash. If it means no more than that, the revolution will fail, in the eyes of Mao Tse-tung and his "activists." Physical transformation of the ancient Chinese earth by collective toil for the benefit of the group and not just for private gain—in a land which was second to none in the pursuit of personal aggrandizement and the devil take the hindmost—is itself so radical a concept and practice that it cannot but create a new philosophy and "world outlook."

Nowhere did I see a more satisfying example of Mao's axioms, "Out of bad things can be made good things" and "Fight self and serve the people," than in the worn and torn hills of northern Shensi, when I returned to the seat of Pao An county. In 1936 I first entered Pao An when it was the Red Army base after the end of the Long March.[1] Mao Tse-tung had his headquarters in a stone cave, and the Red Army Academy, likewise housed, was headed by General Lin Piao. Civil war was still going on.

[1] See *Red Star Over China, op. cit.*

Pro-Red nationalists led me across no man's land and it then took me three days to walk over the hills and ravines, by devious mountain paths, from Yenan to Pao An.

No foreigner had been seen in Pao An since 1945, and very few since 1937, when Mao moved his "capital" to Yenan and the first Nationalist-Communist civil war ended in a united front against the Japanese invaders. A motor road now reaches into Pao An, which lies about 120 kilometers northwest of Yenan. The roadless badlands I had known were steep and interminable unkempt hills divided by ravines, dry except in flood, with only here and there patches of grain and tumbledown caves. The few peasants wore rags, their untutored urchins ran naked, and salt, needles, thread, and matches were precious commodities. They could scarcely feed themselves when the weather was kind, and they starved when it was not. Guerrilla armies who found refuge here had to open up abandoned or waste land and grow their own crops, between battles—and that was the beginning of transformation.

For the countryside always had a better potential— for corn, millet, pasture land, and orchards—than at first met the eye. Part of that potential has now been realized, and the regenerated green-clad hills and narrow valleys are often breathtakingly beautiful.

The motor road, part of a network which leads on into Inner Mongolia, was built for trucks, jeeps, and carts. The appearance of a passenger car brought all within hailing distance to greet us, and the quiet hills seemed suddenly to sprout smiling children to cry, "Long live Chairman Mao!" as we drove past. Cut from steep yellow clay and occasional stone cliffs, which rose precipitously from a deep ravine, the road had slipped away here and there under recent rains. In such places work teams had been mobilized by radio to do quick repair jobs. They simply dug a layer or two deeper into the loess-soil roadbed, and used the earth to strengthen the retaining walls.

As the valley widened we began to see the results of the land reclamation—hills with their tops cut off, garden-like terraces making giant steps down impossible slopes, new rock walls encroaching on the sprawling river course, and rank upon rank of poplars and willows planted to bring the stream under firm control and win precious new valley land. Herds of goats and fat-tailed sheep (three to a household, I was told) grazed along the hilltops.

Fortunately the earth here is worth the torturous effort. "Loess" land is very rich and deep topsoil, blown down from the Gobi Desert in centuries past. On such slopes bulldozers would be useless, and there are none; here all is done by hand. To make just one such man-made ter-race, covering one-third of an acre of useful farmland, I learned, required 20,000 baskets of earth carried on people's backs.

We reached Pao An in about two hours and found the little valley town crowded with more people than I ever saw in one place (apart from troops) in all my months of travel hereabouts in 1936. Then there were scarcely a hundred civilians living in the decrepit county seat; now it held 3,000. The Reds had used a tiny family temple for their mass meetings. Now a theater with a thousand seats advertised *The Red Lantern*, a new-style Peking opera. There had been no industry at all; now there were thirteen handicraft works, a machine repair shop, and a power plant. In 1936 I saw only one store in the whole county. Now a main street was lined with miniature shops. In a small department store we found much the same variety of goods sold everywhere, plus a large wall poster with detailed instructions about how to prepare for air raids.

Li Shih-pin, vice-chairman of the revolutionary com-mittee, welcomed us to a new government headquarters of small clean buildings and guest houses, set beside the river. An open-air feast was spread and we ate with cadres and farmers who had helped produce it: huge ears of corn on the cob, delicious yams, hot-spiced chicken and pork, rice done Shensi style, and a variety of luscious local fruit.

21

The Rich and the Poor

Reclamation work at Pao An was as difficult as at Ta Chai, the famous commune in neighboring Shansi province, now hailed as a national model. "Learn from Ta Chai," said Mao Tse-tung. After twenty-five years of back-breaking toil, leveling hills, and building many miles of stone retaining walls to hold reservoirs, Ta Chai brigade now produces about eight metric tons of grain per hectare. (Its peasant chairman, Ch'en Yung-kuei, is a member of the Party Central Committee, but still works in the fields.)

Equally impressive was the story of the prosperous commune brigade I saw, more than a thousand kilometers east and north of Pao An, and not far from the sea, called Sandstone Gulch. The old inhabitants were a few sans-culotte families who formerly descended on Tangshan or Tientsin every winter to beg coppers or garbage until they could return to the Gulch. After liberation, and with minimal help from the state—they began with seventeen donkeys—the original seventy-eight families year by year dug into the sandstone hills to plant trees and crops. Going very deep, they found water and excavated reservoirs stone-lined by nature.

In 1970 Sandstone Gulch's now 127 households harvested 225 tons of grain and 115 tons of apples, peaches, pears, grapes, dates, and walnuts from their once barren ridges, now held together by woodlands and terraces. On just one hill a hundred men spent ten days to carry earth to and create only *one-sixth* of an acre. By such means Sandstone Gulch now has more than 200 acres of semi-irrigated land. Its stout houses of many-colored stones—dug up in making wells and pools and also used for its clean stone streets—are among the best peasant dwellings in China.

One more example. In Shanghai communes—the Shanghai Special Administrative Area includes ten rural counties—I found brigades digging trenches three meters deep in which to bury huge cement pipes, connected by pumping stations, to replace the surface canals. They thereby add about 8 percent to their precious tillable acreage. A three-year labor project, made by slack-time brigade labor using brigade-made cement pipes, it will also serve, they claim, as emergency air-raid shelters.

22

Looking Backward and Ahead

To review the long and sometimes bloody struggle to collectivize rural China would require a book in itself. Briefly, the postrevolutionary development went from land confiscation and uneven division into small plots (1950); to mutual-aid teams (1950-51); to simple cooperatives, with deeds still privately held (1951-53); to advanced cooperatives, when deeds were burned and villages pooled their land and tools (1955-57); and on to the communes, in 1958, which organized village groups into brigades to undertake large joint projects—canals, roads, dams, industries, schools, hospitals—such as smaller units could not build.

In each phase rich peasants arose and "the spontaneous desire to become a capitalist" was fought down with the support of the poor and middle peasant majority. Old landlord-usurer mentality revived; former landowners attempted comebacks, sabotaged, were put down, arose again, and were beaten back by ceaseless propaganda and organized indoctrination. But mainly the reaction was suppressed by Party leaders able to demonstrate, to a bankrupt peasantry in a country with less than half an acre of usable land per person, that there was no other way to sustained growth beneficial to all than by building collective capital through ceaseless, self-reliant, collective labor.

A great crisis of faith and practice came during the "hardship years," 1959-62. Party cadres leading both the communes and the Great Leap Forward overreached themselves in zeal, haste, and inexperience. Unprecedentedly bad weather then descended before adjustments could be made. Worse than the natural catastrophes, Soviet Russia in 1960 suddenly tore up more than 300 contracts for large-scale industrial and public works, withdrew all her advisers and even spare parts and factory blueprints, and cut China adrift.

To meet the emergency the Party made corrections and offered mild concessions to private enterprise. The commune superstructure was reduced in size and power, many basic responsibilities were returned to the village production teams. It took four years to pick up the pieces of the unfinished industries abandoned by the Russians, and to make up losses in grain output. It was only in 1964 that China caught up with figures claimed for 1958 harvests. Some Party cadres had experimented with a system of greater bonuses and free trade in side lines, production quotas fixed for individual families, and even promises of private ownership of land reclaimed for crops or orchards —a last chance for the rise of a kulak owning class in league with an urban elite.

So Mao Tse-tung saw it. In 1962 he responded, first in the army, and then in the communes, with the Socialist Education Movement, whose goal was to reverse "the spontaneous desire to become a capitalist." When the Great Proletarian Cultural Revolution burst upon the cities, in 1966, the communes were already largely purged of those cadres who had pushed what is now called the "Liu Shao-ch'i line" of individual gain at the expense of the group. The battle was then joined between the urban "capitalist roaders" versus the Marxist line—Mao

Tse-tung Thought—of uncompromising building for an egalitarian society.

Agricultural economy was less affected by the cultural revolution than industry, and rural society gained by heavy injections of urban-educated youth, talent, zeal, and services, aimed to erase differences between city and village. Not until 1970 did China's grain output top 240 million metric tons, a figure still 10 million below the target set for 1962 by the Second (1958-62) Five-Year Plan. In addition China claimed reserves of 40 million tons, although that figure only about equaled imports of foreign grain in the decade 1960-70. The 1970 crop was a net gain on 1950 output of 100 percent, or a growth of about 5 percent a year over the twenty-year period. Well above population growth (about 2 percent a year), 1970 output was double China's grain output of 1950.

Over all China the crop averaged only 2.4 tons per hectare, but communes with yields of up to 8 tons or more per hectare were not uncommon. Two whole provinces—Chekiang and Kwangtung—for the first time averaged 7.5 tons per hectare, well above "green miracle" results reported abroad.

China is today self-sufficient in grain, and future growth will increasingly emphasize "cash crops" for export, to finance rural industrialization and mechanization. With the foundations well laid now there are, as Dr. Chang earlier remarked, "broad vistas in the country-side." Countless difficulties lie ahead, but the "vistas" are real enough, as town and city meet to join farmer, worker, and intellectual in a one-class society, to keep China fully occupied with peaceful works—carried out in a revolutionary way—till the year 2000.

Part Six

A Night with the Premier

23

Chou En-lai
and the Open Door

In two long dialogues Premier Chou En-lai discussed
with me some of China's foreign and domestic policies
and achievements, and released for publication the most
detailed interview he has given for some years. One
session bought forth the first concrete figures on China's
industrial and agricultural output made available in
Peking for nearly a decade.

We sat in a spacious, vaulted, noiseless reception
chamber in the Great Hall of the People. The Premier
was, as usual, urbane, relaxed and alert. A stranger would
hardly have guessed that he was seventy-two and in his
twenty-first year as Premier of the People's Republic, the
last five years of which saw him at the center of stability,
holding an administration together during the second or
cultural revolution.

Behind China's current achievements in broadening
international diplomatic and trade ties there was a
recovered rhythm of agricultural and industrial production following her emergence from a valley of discord.
Considering the depth of that radical upheaval and the
still uncompleted reconstitution of a new state superstructure, it was striking to learn from the Premier that

the basic economy suffered relatively mild damage. "As a result of some struggles in factories, disruption of traffic, and lost labor hours, industrial production in 1967 and 1968 did decline somewhat," he frankly conceded. Without minimizing past difficulties he asserted: "We can still say that what we gained"—in purification of the leadership and revolutionary growth—"was far, far more than we lost."

The Premier said that despite the 1967-68 decline, the goals set for the 1966-70 Five-Year Plan had been basically attained and some had even been greatly exceeded. I asked for an estimate of total value of industrial production in 1970. "Approximately ninety billion U. S. dollars," he answered. "That only includes industry and transportation and does not include commerce and the service trades."

As for agriculture, the Premier said that "as a result of Liu Shao-ch'i's interference" mistakes were made in the late fifties and other mistakes were made in measures of correction during the "hardship years" of 1959-62. "Now for nine years our agriculture has had a steady growth."

He continued: "China's total grain output in 1970 was more than 240 million tons. In addition China has now accumulated state grain reserves of about 40 million tons." Grain tonnage is taken by Western economists as an index of Chinese agricultural conditions. Until recently many of them have continued to regard 1957 as the peak year, when output was officially given as 180 million tons. After that, "buoyant exaggeration" in 1958 greatly distorted China's statistical credibility. Since then few responsible estimates were ventured. The Premier's statement was therefore highly significant.

"If you now have surpluses, why does China continue to import wheat from abroad?"

Although China's grain imports in 1970 dropped to less than 1 percent of her total production, the Premier explained why a limited amount of wheat intake from abroad was necessary. Imported wheat is cheaper in China than rice. China keeps the cheaper wheat for home consumption or reserves and exports rice, in balance, to Cuba and Ceylon in exchange for sugar and rubber, for example, and uses it in African trade. China also sends millions of tons of rice to help Vietnam and other countries.

Premier Chou gave the present production figure for chemical fertilizer as approximately 14 million tons, now considerably above Japanese output. Agriculture here needs 30 to 35 million tons and that is China's goal for 1975, the last year of the new Five-Year Plan. "Thirty million tons of chemical fertilizer may be more or less sufficient but we need more because not only grain crops but cash crops need fertilizer. We still don't have enough phosphates and urea; our chemical fertilizer plants are mainly ammonium sulphate. Small chemical fertilizer plants have been highly effective. We have made big strides on the road to self-sufficiency by building such small plants."

The Premier noted that China had attained the world's largest output of cotton, cotton yarn, and cotton cloth. In 1970 China produced 8.5 billion meters of cotton cloth.

Steel output was also affected by revolutionary struggles in 1967 and 1968, he said. The average production was 10 to 18 million tons during the past five years. Capacity was now being expanded and modernized and might show a rapid increase in 1971.

Oil output reached more than 20 million tons in 1970—self-sufficiency in terms of China's demands. Many new fields had been discovered. Railway mileage and double-tracking had been greatly extended. In southwest China a new and difficult system had been completed, which now connected the frontiers of Vietnam with Sinkiang in Central Asia.

The Premier put agricultural product value for 1970 at about 25 percent of total combined output value of industry, transportation, and agriculture. Calculated on that basis, China's industrial-transportation-agricultural output value in 1970 was around 120 billion American dollars. There is, however, no reliable index for converting "output value" in China in terms of gross national product systems used in the West. "Output value" omits or minimizes important "service values" such as rents, privately owned rural homes—now rising by the millions, built with mutual labor—as well as major and small water conservancy projects constructed by army and volunteer labor. Or consider China's nationwide urban and rural air-raid shelter system, built largely by unpaid neighborhood mutual labor teams. It would elsewhere cost billions of dollars. Finally, how is one to fit into the GNP formula the value of thirty million acres of marginal land added during the past ten years to the cultivable area by peasant labor—with unbelievable toil—at a cost of little more than peasant food consumption?

China's output figures are based on a constant-value yuan, fixed at a rate of 2.40 to the U. S. dollar since 1953. Until now China has avoided inflation, internal prices have remained stable and on many items have been reduced, while low wages have risen more in purchasing power than in cash. China has no internal or external debt, the Premier proudly pointed out. There is no personal income tax and basic consumer necessities are generally cheaper, amazingly so in food, now available in variety and abundance, as any visitor to China may see for himself.

Taking various imponderables into account, one is tempted to suggest a hypothetical GNP for China much nearer to that of the larger West European countries than is generally supposed. The hard fact remains that in per capita income China still ranks among the poorer countries, with its population, despite mass birth control measures, approaching 800 million.

Switching to internal politics, the Premier discussed

some features which he felt were misrepresented abroad. Although at one time it was widely reported that the entire Communist Party was dissolved during the cultural revolution, membership was in fact only suspended and the Premier now asserted that less than 1 percent was expelled. In echelons of higher leadership changes were of course much greater. At the Ninth Party Congress held in 1969, for example, a large majority of the former membership of the Central Committee and the former Politburo was replaced by cadres who had emerged from the cultural revolution. Yet the majority of those not reelected had not been expelled from the Party but had gone down to the countryside to "temper themselves," according to Chou.

Under Mao Tse-tung's leadership the Party and the state superstructure were now being rebuilt throughout the country. Councils or congresses of peasants, workers, mass organizations, and the People's Liberation Army were preparing to send delegates to a new National People's Congress. Its purpose would be to adopt a new constitution to affirm the character of the new state, and the form of future central and local government, as well as the people's fundamental rights and duties.[1]

That the rural communes continued to sow and reap better harvests, that industry recovered and advanced in new technologies, and that government and Party did not disintegrate into anarchy during the cultural revolution: all that was attributable, said the Premier, to the people's unity and faith in the teachings and leadership of Mao Tse-tung. That fact would now be explicitly recognized in the new constitution. It would state that "the People's Republic of China is led by Mao Tse-tung, and the Thought of Mao Tse-tung is the guiding principle of all our work." It would also "openly declare" the prole-

[1] As of early 1972, the draft state constitution had not yet been approved by the National People's Congress.

tarian state to be irrevocably under the leadership of the Communist Party.

Likewise in the constitution, said Chou, would be guarantees of new forms created by the people during the cultural revolution for carrying out the socialist revolution: the right "freely to air their views; to arouse the masses; to engage in great debates; and to write *ta tzu-pao.*" The constitution would also guarantee the right to strike, Premier Chou added.

One point the Premier wished to be clearly understood. The foreign press had greatly misinterpreted the role of the army by presenting it as dominating both the Party and the government. That had not been and would never be the case, he said; in the future it would become even further evident to those who wished to analyze the Party leadership.

Between interviews with the Premier and other officials, my wife and I traveled about the country above and below the Great Wall, retracing some of my old paths and exploring new ones. We met people at work in farming communes and on local industries—in urban communes and their revived neighborhood workshops—in large modern industries cooperating with schools and in universities experimenting with innovations in teaching and in student selection. We visited hospitals where modern surgery is combined with acupuncture and training of the village medicine men called barefoot doctors. We visited a commune where whole families, down to age six, engaged in target practice; we met teachers and actors and high officials laboring in rice paddies and saying they liked it; and we saw electricians demonstrating how to repair overhead wires, alive with 220,000 volts, before spectators who included the director of China's largest steel plant and the chairman of a governing revolutionary committee in a city of a million men.

We found Premier Chou interested in our impressions of the cultural revolution and eager for fresh news of the

United States. That I was the first American writer to return to China to gather material for Western publications perhaps in itself gave significance to these interviews. The major obstacle to reopening long-closed lines of communication between the Chinese and American peoples remained, as for nearly two decades, the United States' armed protectorate over Taiwan and Chiang Kai-shek's defeated Nationalist regime there.

The Premier reviewed the new condition in China's world relationships, featured by her expanding trade and diplomatic ties with foreign states, notably increased since Canadian and Italian recognition. Not surprisingly it was believed in the People's Republic that continuing diplomatic breakthroughs, including the changing vote to seat China in the United Nations, would increasingly isolate the Taiwan regime and isolate the United States and Japan over the Taiwan question in the world community. The "revolt" was now becoming general, the Premier observed, reaching to all continents. Even in Western Europe few countries were left which still had relations with Chiang Kai-shek. Canadian and Italian recognition had ended illusions about the viability of a "two-China" compromise, or a "one China, one Taiwan" arrangement.

"What will be China's response whenever the United Nations votes in favor of recognizing the People's Republic as entitled to China's seat in the Security Council?" Premier Chou replied: "And with Chiang's clique out of the United Nations altogether? Then, of course we would consider that. The future of the United Nations is hard to predict. There are two possibilities. One possibility is that [organizational] change will take place. The other is that it may suffer the same fate as the League of Nations. It becomes evident from the twenty-fifth session of the General Assembly that an increasing number of medium and small countries and even certain big countries are opposing the superpowers' manipulation of the United

Nations, or, more often, bypassing the United Nations to play power politics, divide spheres of influence, and even scramble for high seas and space."

In this part of the world China was still threatened with war by the superpowers, Chou asserted: with some one million Soviet land, air, and naval forces as well as rocket troops to the north and west; and with the United States in alliance with a remilitarizing Japan on the east, and through Taiwan even deeper into Southeast Asia.

Since Taiwan is Chinese territory, United States encroachment there was regarded as the crux of Sino-American difference which led to the Indochina war, where China had now extended an umbrella of protection and support to the alliance of the three Indochinese peoples against the United States. The Premier recalled that in 1960 and 1964 he had spelled out for me the conditions under which the Taiwan problem could be solved so as to establish Sino-American relations.[2] He said that there had been and would be no change. China required that 1) the United States must recognize Taiwan as an inalienable part of the People's Republic of China and must withdraw all its armed forces from Taiwan and the Taiwan Straits; 2) despite their different social systems, China and the United States should practice peaceful coexistence on the basis of the Five Principles.

"Taiwan is China's internal affair and the Chinese people alone have the right to liberate it. United States armed aggression there is another question, an international question, and we are ready to negotiate that," Premier Chou said. "The door is open but it depends on whether the United States is serious in dealing with the Taiwan question." He expressed friendly feelings for the American people. He indicated a readiness to consider

[2] For text of the 1964 interviews, see Appendix, Talks with Chou En-lai. For 1960 interviews see *Red China Today, op. cit.*

applications from "friends of China, in concrete cases, and in a concrete way," to visit here.

Chou En-lai explained the Chinese side of the present deadlock in Sino-Soviet boundary negotiations, which had persisted for more than a year. On September 11, 1969, the Chinese and Soviet premiers reached an understanding that Sino-Soviet boundary negotiations should be held free from any threat and that the two sides would reach an agreement on provisional measures to maintain the status quo of the border, avert armed conflicts, and disengage the armed forces of both sides in disputed areas. "Disputed areas," according to Premier Chou, are places where the two sides differ in their boundary delineations on the maps, according to the Sino-Russian boundary treaties of the nineteenth century: "That is to say, they are places which they say belong to them and we say belong to us. This question can be solved only when an agreement on the provisional measures has been reached and adjustment is to be made in accordance with the principles of mutual understanding, mutual accommodation, and consultations on an equal footing. And it really shouldn't be difficult to settle."

In practice, it seemed, the Russians had simply refused to agree to disengage in the disputed areas, where the two lines remained, as intertwined as the prongs of two forks pushed together.

I asked the Premier whether he would today repeat China's call, made in the early 1960s, for a summit conference to prohibit the use of nuclear weapons, to abolish their manufacture, and to secure their total destruction.

"Let me make our position on this question clear," he replied. "In the first place, our nuclear tests are still in the experimental stage, and every test carried out is limited and made only when necessary. The aim of our nuclear tests is to break the nuclear monopoly and nuclear blackmail and prevent a nuclear war. Therefore, each time when we conduct a test, we declare that at no time and in no circumstances shall China be the first to use nuclear weapons. And we reiterate the proposal that a summit conference of all countries of the world, big or small, be convened to conclude an agreement on the complete prohibition and thorough destruction of nuclear weapons and, as the first step, to reach an agreement to prohibit the use of nuclear weapons. After our recent test (October 14, 1970) the Japanese Socialist Party expressed their support for this stand and proposal of ours."

As for "so-called nuclear arms limitation" talks between the superpowers, he said, these were aimed to maintain their monopoly over all others, and nothing else. Each power concentrated only on how to "limit" the other so as to maintain its own superiority. The United States and the Soviet Union indeed wished to "limit" the costs of supporting their monopoly of terror, but the costs nevertheless continued to rise astronomically even as they talked. As to how their contradictions were ever to be resolved, "We are not their chiefs of staff!" He said, "Don't cherish any illusion in that kind of 'disarmament.' For twenty-five years they have all along been engaged in arms expansion, and not at all disarmament."

Speaking of China's "world outlook," Premier Chou quoted Chairman Mao's words: "The people of all countries, the masses comprising more than 90 percent of the entire population, sooner or later want revolution. . . ." According to Chairman Mao, he said, the danger of a world war still existed, and the people of all countries must be prepared. But "revolution is the main trend in the world today."

The Premier said that Chairman Mao's statement of May 20, 1970, foresaw prospects for an American revolution. Indeed, no one could speak seriously to responsible Chinese leaders without noticing their intense interest in the signs they detected of disintegration of American capitalist society. Clearly Chairman Mao was not expecting an early American revolution, however, nor seeking to build China's foreign policy on that speculation. The policy for which China sought adherence was more limited. It called not only for American troops to be withdrawn from Asia and Taiwan, but also for all foreign troops "to be withdrawn from all territories they are occupying, and go home, so that people of all countries may enjoy the right to solve their problems on their own without any menace or interference from the outside."

My own impression after nearly six months in China was that the recovery of political stability and economic growth was now a first priority, while abroad China sought the renewal and expansion of state-to-state ties on the basis of the old Bandung principles of peaceful coexistence. China did not aspire to become a nuclear superpower but aimed at credible deterrent power while seeking to end superpower domination in world affairs with the cooperation of the medium and small powers. Relying on her own means, however, China had never been so well prepared for war, and to frustrate American military and political purposes in Asia by fulfilling her obligations to support Hanoi and the Indochinese peoples allied with Hanoi.

Part Seven

*Breakfast
with the Chairman*

24

A Conversation
with Mao Tse-tung

Chairman Mao emphasized that he did not wish to be interviewed. What we had was a conversation. I later confirmed, however, that he would not object to publication of certain of his comments without the use of direct quotation. During most of our talk, on December 18, 1970, notes were taken by Nancy T'ang, American-born daughter of T'ang Ming-chao. (Mr. T'ang was editor of the *Overseas Chinese Daily* in New York until 1949. Since then he had served in China as a leader of cultural and political relations with foreign countries.) One other person was present—a Chinese woman secretary. It was interesting that neither of the young women wore a Mao badge: this was the only occasion on which I met an official when the badge was not on display.

I recorded our dialogue from memory immediately afterward and also was given a copy of Miss T'ang's notes.

Chairman Mao's residence in Peking lies in the southwestern corner of the former Forbidden City, surrounded by vermilion walls and not far from the T'ien An Men, or Heavenly Peace Gate, where he reviews the October anniversary parade. Behind these high walls, topped by glistening yellow tiles, the old imperial regime also

housed its officials. Today members of the Politburo live
and work here in close proximity to the Chairman and
Premier Chou En-lai. One enters through the West Gate,
flanked by two armed guards. Circling around an empty
wooded drive, one quickly comes to a one-story dwelling
of modest size, built in traditional style.

At the entrance one is greeted by two unarmed officers,
who wear no insignia of rank. "They are generals," con-
fides Nancy T'ang. How does she know? They disappear
when the Chairman meets me at the door of his study. I
apologize for keeping him waiting. I had been asleep
when summoned without advance notice.

It was early morning. We had breakfast together and
talked until about one o'clock. He was slightly indis-
posed with a cold and he wondered out loud what doctors
were good for: they could not even prevent a simple
disease like colds, which cost so much lost time. I mentioned Dr. Linus Pauling—he had heard of him—and his
advocacy of large doses of ascorbic acid as a cold pana-
cea. I offered to send him some. He said he would try it.
If it helped I would get the credit. If it poisoned him I
would not be blamed.

Mao's large study was completely lined with shelves
filled by hundreds of Chinese books, with a sprinkling of
foreign volumes. From many of them dangled slips of
paper used as annotated bookmarks. The large desk was
piled high with journals and scripts. It was a working
writer's shop. Through the wide windows one could catch
a glimpse of garden where the Chairman was said to
grow his own vegetables and experiment with crops. It is
not a "private plot"; it belongs to the state. Perhaps he
needed the output, since he was said to have taken a
recent cut of 20 percent in his subsistence "wages."

We discussed my account of our last talk, in January,
1965,[1] in which I had reported his acknowledgment that

[1] For complete text of that interview, see Appendix, *South of the
Mountains to North of the Seas.*

there was indeed a "cult of personality" in China—and moreover there was reason for one. Some people had criticized me for writing about that.

So, he said, what if I had written about a "cult of personality" in China? There was such a thing. Why not write about it? It was a fact . . . those officials who had opposed my return to China in 1967 and 1968 had belonged to an ultraleftist group which had seized the Foreign Ministry for a time, but they were all cleared out long ago. At the time of our 1965 colloquy, Mao continued, a great deal of power—over propaganda work within the provincial and local party committees, and especially within the Peking Municipal Party Committee—had been out of his control. That was why he had then stated that there was need for more personality cult, in order to stimulate the masses to dismantle the anti-Mao Party bureaucracy.

Of course the personality cult had been overdone. Today, things were different. It was hard, the Chairman said, for people to overcome the habits of 3,000 years of emperor-worshiping tradition. The so-called "Four Greats"—those epithets applied to Mao himself: "Great Teacher, Great Leader, Great Supreme Commander, Great Helmsman"—what a nuisance. They would all be eliminated sooner or later. Only the word "teacher" would be retained—that is, simply schoolteacher. Mao had always been a schoolteacher and still was one. He was a primary schoolteacher in Changsha even before he was a Communist. All the rest of the titles would be declined.

"Sometimes I wonder," I said, "whether those who shout Mao the loudest and wave the most banners are not—as some say—waving the Red Flag in order to defeat the Red Flag."

Mao nodded. He said such people fell into three categories. The first were sincere people. The second were those who drifted with the tide—they conformed because everyone else shouted "Long live!" ("*Wansui!*") The third category was insincere. I must not be taken in by such stuff.

"I remember," I said, "that just before you entered Peking in 1949 the Central Committee adopted a resolution—reportedly at your suggestion—which forbade naming streets, cities, or places for anybody."

Yes, he said, they had avoided that; but other forms of worship had emerged. There were so many slogans. Pictures and plaster statues. The Red Guard had insisted that if you didn't have those things around, you were being anti-Mao. In the past few years there had been need for some personality cult. Now there was no such need and there should be a cooling down.

But after all, he went on, did not the Americans have their own personality cult? How could the governor of each state, how could each President and each cabinet member, get along without some people to worship them? There was always the desire to be worshiped and the desire to worship. Could you, he asked me, be happy if no one read your books and articles? There was bound to be some worship of the individual and that applied to me too.

Chairman Mao had obviously pondered very much over this phenomenon—the human need for and to worship, about gods and God. On earlier visits he had discussed it at length. Now, at seventy-six, he was in general good health but once again he said that he would "soon be going to see God." It was inevitable; everyone eventually had to see God.

"Voltaire wrote that if there were no God it would be necessary for man to invent one," I said. "If he had expressed himself as an outright atheist it might have cost him his head, in those times."

Mao agreed that many people had lost their heads for saying much less.

"We have made some progress since then," I said. "And

man has been able to change God's views on a number of things. One of them is birth control; about that, there is a great change here in China compared with five or ten years ago."

No, he said. I had been taken in! In the countryside a woman still wanted to have boy children. If the first ones were girls, she would continue trying. . . . The attitude must be changed but it was taking time. Perhaps the same thing was true in the United States?

"China is ahead in that respect," I said. "A women's liberation movement in the United States is making some impact, however. American women were the first to achieve the vote and they are now learning how to use it."

At this point we were interrupted by the arrival of some glasses of *mao t'ai*, a fiery rice liquor made in Kweichow province. We drank a toast. To my mortification the Chairman noticed that I had omitted to toast the ladies present. How could I have done so? I had not yet accepted women as equals.

It was not possible, said the Chairman, to achieve complete equality between men and women at present. But between Chinese and Americans there need be no prejudices. There could be mutual respect and equality. He said he placed high hopes on the peoples of the two countries.

If the Soviet Union wouldn't do (point the way), then he would place his hopes on the American people. The United States alone had a population of more than 200 million. Industrial production was already higher than in any other country, and education was universal. He would be happy to see a party emerge there to lead a revolution, although he was not expecting that in the near future.

In the meantime, he said, the Foreign Ministry was studying the matter of admitting Americans from the left, middle, and right to visit China. Should rightists like

Nixon, who represented the monopoly capitalists, be permitted to come? He should be welcomed because, Mao explained, at present the problems between China and the U.S.A. would have to be solved with Nixon. Mao would be happy to talk with him, either as a tourist or as President.

I, unfortunately, could not represent the United States, he said; I was not a monopoly capitalist. Could *I* settle the Taiwan question? Why continue such a stalemate? Chiang Kai-shek had not died yet. But what had Taiwan to do with Nixon? That question was created by Truman and Acheson.

It may be relevant to mention—and this was not a part of my talk with Chairman Mao—that foreign diplomats in Peking had been aware that messages were being delivered from Washington to the Chinese government by certain go-betweens. The purport of such communications was to assure Chinese leaders of Mr. Nixon's "new outlook" on Asia. Nixon was firmly determined, it was said, to withdraw from Vietnam as speedily as possible, to seek a negotiated international guarantee of the independence of Southeast Asia, to end the impasse in Sino-American relations by clearing up the Taiwan question and to bring the People's Republic into the United Nations and into diplomatic relations with the United States.

Two important Frenchmen were in China in 1970. The first was André Bettencourt, the minister of planning, the second was Maurice Couve de Murville, premier under De Gaulle's regime. M. Couve de Murville completed arrangements for a visit to China by General de Gaulle which was to have occurred this year. It was to General de Gaulle, I was authoritatively informed, that Mr. Nixon had first confided his intention to seek a genuine détente with China. Some people had anticipated that De Gaulle, during his visit, would play a key role in promoting serious Sino-American conversations. Death ruled otherwise.

Chairman Mao's tribute to the General, sent to Mme. de Gaulle, was the only eulogy which he was known to have offered for any non-Communist statesman since Roosevelt died.

Meanwhile, other diplomats had been active. The head of one European mission in Peking, who had already made one trip to see President Nixon, returned to Washington last December. He bypassed the State Department to confer at the White House, and was back in China in January. From another and unimpeachable diplomatic source I learned, not long before my departure from Peking in February, that the White House had once more conveyed a message asking how a personal representative of the President would be received in the Chinese capital for conversations with the highest Chinese leaders. About the same time, I was enigmatically told by a senior Chinese diplomat who had formerly maintained quite the opposite, "Nixon is getting out of Vietnam."

I must once more stress that none of the above background information was provided to me by Mao Tse-tung.

As we talked, the Chairman recalled to me once again that it was the Japanese militarists who had taught revolution to the Chinese people. Thanks to their invasion, they had provoked the Chinese people to fight and had helped bring Chinese socialism to power.

I mentioned how Prince Sihanouk had told me a few days before that "Nixon is the best agent for Mao Tse-tung. The more he bombs Cambodia, the more Communists he makes. He is their best ammunition carrier," said the Prince. Yes, Mao agreed. He liked that kind of help.

I reminded him that when I had spoken to him two months before, during the October Day parade at T'ien An Men Square, he had told me that he was "not satisfied with the present situation." I asked him to explain what he meant.

He replied that there were two things of which he

highly disapproved during the cultural revolution. One was lying. Someone, while saying that the struggle should be carried out by reasoning, not by coercion or force, actually gave the other fellow a kick under the table and then drew back his leg. When the person kicked asked, "Why did you kick me?" the first person said, "I didn't kick you. Don't you see my foot is still here?" That, Mao said, is lying. Later the conflict during the cultural revolution developed into war between factions—first with spears, then rifles, then mortars. When foreigners reported that China was in great chaos, they had not been telling lies. It had been true. Fighting was going on.

The other thing the Chairman was most unhappy about was the maltreatment of "captives"—Party members and others removed from power and subjected to reeducation. The old practice of the Liberation Army—freeing captives and giving them fares to go home, which resulted in many enemy soldiers being moved to volunteer and join their ranks—had often been ignored. Maltreatment of captives now had slowed the rebuilding and transformation of the Party.

If one did not speak the truth, Mao concluded, how could he gain the confidence of others? Who would trust one? The same applied between friends.

"Are the Russians afraid of China?" I asked.

Some people said so, he replied, but why should they be? China's atom bomb was only this size (Mao raised his little finger), while Russia's bomb was that size (he raised his thumb). Together the Russian and American bombs were (putting two thumbs together) that size. What could a little finger do against two thumbs?

"But from the long-range view. Do the Russians fear China?"

It was said that they were a bit afraid, he answered. Even when there are a few mice in a person's room the person could become frightened, fearful that the mice might eat up his sweets. For instance, the Russians were upset because China was building air-raid shelters. But if the Chinese got into their shelters, how could they attack others?

As for ideology, who had fired the first shot? The Russians had called the Chinese dogmatists and then the Chinese had called them revisionists. China had published their criticisms, but the Russians had not dared publish China's. Then they had sent some Cubans and later Romanians to ask the Chinese to cease open polemics. That would not do, Mao said. The polemics would have to be carried on for 10,000 years if necessary. Then Kosygin himself had come. After their talk Mao had told him that he would take off 1,000 years but no more.

The Russians looked down on the Chinese and also looked down on the people of many countries, he said. They thought that they only had to speak the word and all people would listen and obey. They did not believe that there were people who would not do so and that one of them was his humble self. Although Sino-Russian ideological differences were now irreconcilable—as demonstrated by their contradictory policies in Cambodia—they could eventually settle their problems as between states.

Referring once again to the United States, Chairman Mao said that China should learn from the way America developed, by decentralizing and spreading responsibility and wealth among the fifty states. A central government could not do everything. China must depend upon regional and local initiatives. It would not do (spreading his hands) to leave everything up to him.

As he courteously escorted me to the door, he said he was not a complicated man, but really very simple. He was, he said, only a lone monk walking the world with a leaky umbrella.

As a result of this and other informal conversations, I believed that in future Sino-American talks, Chairman

Mao would surely adhere to the basic principles which had guided China in all her foreign policies, her ideological and world view as well as her regional policies. On the other hand, I also believed that, following an easing of international tensions, China would seek to cooperate with all friendly states, and all friendly people within hostile states, who welcomed her full participation in world affairs.

Part Eight

Nixon's Reach
for the Forbidden City

Shoe display: prices here range from $2 to $10 (felt-soled cotton shoes start at a dollar) / A specialty food store in Peking / 16 HP Diesel engines, made in Shanghai for use in the countryside HSIN HUA

Mealtime at a factory; steamed rolls for lunch

China-made "Phoenix" sedans in a Shanghai factory

Ceramic factory worker   *A high-school student worker*

A three-wheeled truck, popular in rural areas

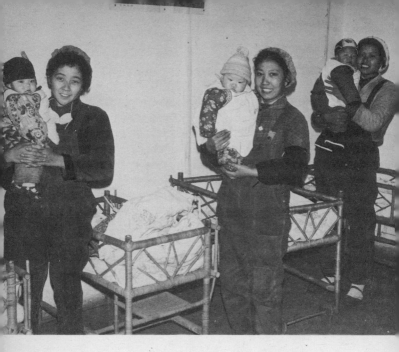

Nursing mothers in the day nursery of a diesel engine factory, Wusih. There is also a birth control clinic on the premises

Acupuncture is the anesthetic for most abortions

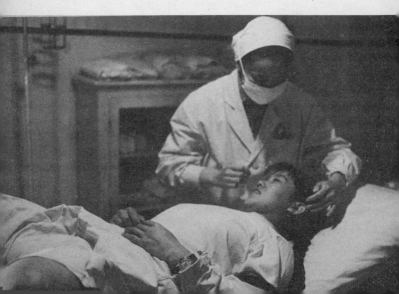

A barefoot doctor at Hsin-Hsua, a flower commune near Canton

Physiotherapy in a workers' rehabilitation clinic

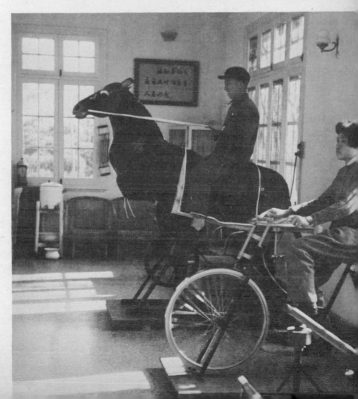

Young Pioneers in front of one of China's new-built air raid shelters

Playground scene in Pei Hai Park, Peking

Improvised ping-pong match in a renovation project

Early morning in Min Hong, a new housing development near Shanghai

Family in front of their home, Yellow Ridge commune

Edgar and Lois
Wheeler Snow at
Yenan, outside Mao's
1936 cave headquarters,
1970

Edgar Snow with
Mao Tse-tung, 1965

Rewi Alley, Dr. and
Mrs. George Hatem,
1970

25

A Position of Strength

Many are the answers and speculations offered to explain why President Nixon sought and accepted an invitation to Peking, but why were the Chinese responsive? Was it forgotten in Peking that Nixon built his early career on witch-hunting and climbed to the Senate and vice-presidency on the backs of "appeasers in the State Department" who sold China to Russia? Why should Mao Tse-tung, with a fierce domestic purge safely behind him, seeing America's Vietnam venture a shambles and believing its political and economic position to be in serious trouble abroad and at home, accept a belated olive branch? And if Nixon was not going to China just to eat shark fins, what might his hosts serve as side dishes—and what might they expect in return?

The question about Nixon has been partly answered for us by Chairman Mao in my earlier report.[1] He told me that Nixon, who represented the monopoly capitalists, should be welcomed simply because at present the problems between China and the United States would have to be solved with him. In the dialectical pattern of his thought Mao had often said that good can come out of bad and that bad people can be made good—by experience and right teaching. Yes, he said to me, he preferred men like Nixon to Social Democrats and revisionists, those

[1] See Chapter 24, A Conversation with Mao Tse-tung.

who professed to be one thing but in power behaved quite otherwise.

Nixon might be deceitful, he went on, but perhaps a little bit less so than some others. Nixon resorted to tough tactics but he also used some soft tactics. Yes, Nixon could just get on a plane and come. It would not matter whether the talks would be successful. If he were willing to come, the Chairman would be willing to talk to him and it would be all right. It would be all right, whether or not they quarreled, or whether Nixon came as a tourist or as President. He believed they would not quarrel. But of course he would offer criticism of Nixon. The hosts would also make self-criticism and talk about their own mistakes and shortcomings—for instance, their production level was lower than that of the United States.

What had happened since January, 1965, to change Mao's mind? At that time I had asked the Chairman if there was any message I might deliver to President Johnson, and his answer was *Pu-shih* (No!) and nothing more. Even so, Mao said then that one possible solution to the Vietnam conflict was still a new Geneva conference to end the fighting and guarantee Indochina's independence.[2] That message reached the State Department, but the "option" was almost immediately closed out by Johnson's bombing of North Vietnam.

In that 1965 interview Mao had made it clear enough that he did not expect the Americans to desist until they had learned, the hard way, that they could not impose their political will on revolutionary Vietnam by military violence.

The Chinese believed that the lesson of Vietnam, and no mere change of Presidents, was what made it possible for Mao in 1970 to speak differently about Nixon. "Experience" had made Nixon relatively "good." Other major

---

[2] For complete text of that interview, see Appendix, *South of the Mountains to North of the Seas.*

changes had also altered their view: antiwar resistance inside the United States; the formation of an alliance linking Hanoi, the VC, and resistance forces in Cambodia and Laos, unilaterally backed by Peking. And there had been changes inside China itself, including the sobering growth of nuclear missiles and delivery capacity.

Theoretically, the Chinese believed, Nixon had various options along the way and did make use of them as tactical threats for a time—as in Cambodia and Laos. But the end was near. Once the decision was taken to get out of Vietnam, clearly a U. S. understanding with China became imperative. The President had not only to safeguard his rear against possible destruction by a China-backed North Vietnam offensive, but also to cope with domestic and world political repercussions of withdrawal.

That was the general view in 1970 from the Heavenly Peace Gate, but preparations continued for the worst. (Bad can also come out of good.)

In the summer of 1969, the Nixon Administration had publicly urged an easing of tensions with China; later that year it had stopped the Taiwan Straits patrols, and the Chinese took note, of course. The administration also proposed to resume the suspended Warsaw talks at any mutually agreeable time or place. In January, 1970, preliminary Sino-American talks opened in Warsaw. They were immediately suspended after the Cambodian invasion. But Nixon went ahead, carried out a stage-by-stage elimination of trade embargoes against China, and lifted travel bans between the two countries. Early in the spring a presidential commission advocated a U.N. seat for mainland China, for the first time officially calling it the People's Republic. Peking leaders remained suspicious—especially of a double-cross play between Moscow and Washington.

By late autumn of 1970 several urgent and authentically documented inquiries reaching China had indicated that the President wished to know whether he or his represen-

tative would be received in Peking. An indirect answer
was contained in an interview given to me by Chou En-lai
in November, when he said that Sino-American conversations could be opened but only if the Americans demonstrated a "serious" desire to negotiate.[3] To the initiated,
"serious" meant, first of all, a realistic attempt to work
out a program to deal with the Taiwan problem. As Mao
and Chou saw it, that was the key to all other Asian set-
tlements. Evidently sufficient assurances were forthcoming. When Chou En-lai led my wife and me to stand
beside Chairman Mao's side on October Day, 1970, and to
be photographed at the anniversary parade, no American
had ever been so noticed. Discerning people realized that
something new was happening. Then came the ping-pong
gesture. Chairman Mao had talked to me in December, and
after the ping-pong gesture I was able to report that he
would welcome Mr. Nixon or his personal representative to
Peking. A new horizon was already in sight.

My *Life* article reporting on my conversation with
the Chairman was translated and widely circulated in
China among political and army leaders. They could not,
therefore, have been much astonished by the Peking-
Washington joint announcement. Though China's press
might carry only a few lines, the whole subject was undoubtedly cautiously discussed and explained down to
the commune level. Only one thing may have surprised
the Chinese: Mr. Kissinger's success in keeping his visit
secret. Experience with American diplomats during World
War II had convinced Chinese leaders that Americans
could not keep secrets.

The Chinese were, of course, well aware not only of
the international impact of Mr. Nixon's plans, but also of
the domestic effects and side benefits to his present and
future political career. Discussing Nixon's possible visit
to China, the Chairman casually remarked that the presidential election would be in 1972, would it not? Therefore,

[3] See page 160.

he added, Mr. Nixon might send an envoy first, but was not himself likely to come to Peking before early 1972.

By 1970 China had passed through the ordeal of a great purge, much time had been lost in domestic construction, and many fences had to be mended or newly built to end China's international isolation. The period of internal tension was largely over. Now, if there was a chance to recover Taiwan—Mao's last national goal of unification—and for China to be accepted as an equal in recognition of her great size, achievements, and potential, why not look at it? Nothing in Mao's thought or teaching ever called for a war against the United States or for a war of foreign conquest, and nothing in Mao's ideology placed any faith in nuclear bombs. The burden of building bombs and counterattack silos was very heavy indeed and likely to become more so; China had more than once called for their total abolition.

Very high among the reasons why Sino-American rapprochement interested China was to improve her strategic position in dealing with Russia. With America off the Asian continent, the danger of a Soviet-American gang-up dispelled, and a seat of her own in the U.N., Peking's maneuvering power would obviously be enhanced.

Did Mr. Kissinger understand, then, that China was ready to talk from a position of strength, not weakness? China's leaders respected Kissinger. They knew him through their own intelligence system and through his writing. Discussing him with an old friend and close comrade-in-politics of Premier Chou one evening in Peking, I was struck by his frank delight at the prospect of crossing verbal swords with such a worthy adversary. "Kissinger?" he said. "There is a man who knows the language of both worlds—his own and ours. He is the first American we have seen in his position. With him it should be possible to talk."

The immediate issues examined at the meeting between Chou and Kissinger—and the agenda for the presidential discussion—were very concrete and could scarcely have been anything very new to either side. As the Chinese saw it, solutions would involve these turning-point decisions for Nixon: 1) seating the People's Republic in the United Nations and the return of Taiwan to mainland sovereignty; 2) total U. S. withdrawal from Vietnam and arrangements for an international conference to guarantee Indochina's independence, and for a negotiated Hanoi-Saigon settlement which would preserve some shell of the American-made regime, at least for a decent interval; and 3) the establishment of formal Sino-American diplomatic relations. On all these matters, some rough negotiable script had to be brought back to Nixon to enable him to accept Premier Chou's invitation.

China's formula for Taiwan had always been negotiable whenever American leaders so wished. As repeatedly defined, it required two steps: first, that the U. S. and China jointly declare their intention to settle all disputes between them, including the Taiwan dispute, by peaceful negotiation. Second, that the U. S. recognize Taiwan as an inalienable part of the Chinese People's Republic and agree to withdraw its armed forces from Taiwan and the Taiwan Straits. Specific steps on how and when to withdraw would be matters for subsequent discussion.

China contended that the dispute with the U. S. over Taiwan was an international question whereas her interrupted civil war with Chiang Kai-shek was a strictly internal question. Once American agreement to withdraw from Taiwan was conceded in principle, many terms would have to be defined. Peking was likely to be found reasonable both in the procedures for the dissolution of the American position and in dealing with Taiwan itself— perhaps even granting some autonomy to Chiang Kai-shek if he should wish to remain governor there for his lifetime.

China would never publicly renounce what it considers its ultimate sovereign right to recover Taiwan by force if necessary. However, there was now a likelihood that a non-military solution would be worked out by the Nationalists and the Communist Chinese themselves. The opening of serious Sino-American talks might have already provoked renewed covert conversations between Taiwan and Peking in a search for the possible terms of assimilation. That was no doubt one of Nixon's hopes. Mao Tse-tung pointed out to me that peaceful assimilation of Taiwan was his aim—reminding me of several cases in the Chinese civil war when other provinces acceded without fighting.

A settlement in Taiwan obviously could not be separated, however, from a cease-fire agreement and withdrawal in Vietnam, nor could the latter await the former. Nothing less than total evacuation of all foreign forces from Vietnam would satisfy Peking's Hanoi allies, as indicated by protests already coming from Hanoi and warnings to Peking against Nixon's perfidy. Peking could not permit Russia to exploit differences of this nature, and it was surely made clear to Kissinger that no Geneva conference solution could be advanced by China that did not have the full support of Hanoi and the NLF.

Such were the regional issues that must be settled before any across-the-board détente could be reached in East Asia and the broader Pacific. To define China's less immediate but parallel aspirations on a global scale is beyond the scope of this report, but that they include continued support for revolutionary struggle—"in the interest of China and the whole world"—is obvious.

On his visit to Peking the President would be entering a nation with which his country had no diplomatic relations and one in which the real chief of state held no executive office. Meet the Party Chairman Nixon certainly would, but in all probability Chou would do most of the negotiating.

What sort of man would the President see in Chou En-lai? Clearly one of the world's ablest negotiators. Handsome and exuding charisma, he was, in his seventy-third year, tireless. In August, 1967, Chou negotiated his way out of his most perilous moment in the cultural revolution. Though idolized by youth, he was, for more than two days and nights, surrounded in his offices in the Great Hall by half a million ultraleftist Red Guards. Their leaders—some later arrested as counterrevolutionaries—were seeking to seize the files of the Central Committee—and Chou himself. Mao and Lin Piao were both absent. By talking to small groups, day and night, Chou gradually persuaded the masses—so Chou called them in talking to me—to disperse. It was only following that incident that Lin Piao brought thousands of troops into the capital, and the disarming and breakup of the Red Guards began in earnest—with heavy casualties.

Kissinger is said to have spent twenty of his forty-nine hours in Peking talking to the Premier. That is nothing extraordinary. One of several interview-conversations I had with him lasted from the dinner table one evening until six the next morning. I was exhausted, he seemingly as fresh as ever. "I must let you get some sleep," I mumbled.

He threw back his head and laughed. "I've already had my sleep," he said. "Now I'm going to work." His night's rest had been a catnap before dinner.

Chou told me that he had taken one vacation—a week when he was ill—in ten years.

Carefully avoiding any thrust for personal power, the Premier has been a zestful worker in pursuit of national and revolutionary power politics. His affable manner masks viscera of tough and supple alloys; he is a master of policy implementation with an infinite capacity for detail. His personal contacts are innumerable. He combines an administrative efficiency hard to reconcile with his ubiquity. His self-effacing dedication makes him Mao's indispensable alter ego.

Symbiosis is perhaps the best word to describe their relationship. Very different in working style and personality, Mao and Chou complement each other as a

tandem based on thirty-seven years of trust and inter-
dependence. Chou was never a mandarin but his grandfather was, and he confesses to a feudal background,
although he spent twenty years in peasant surroundings
as a guerrilla. Mao is a peasant-born intellectual genius
to whose intuitive and experienced knowledge of the
people Chou habitually defers.

Mao is an activist, a prime mover, an originator and
master of strategy achieved by alternating surprise, tension, and easement. He distrusts long periods of stability
and is never satisfied with the pace of change, but he is
practical and capable of great patience in achieving a goal
by stages.

Chou welcomes the detailed execution of a plan—which
bores Mao—and the more complex the problem the better.
Chou quickly cuts to the heart of matters, drops the
impractical, dissimulates when necessary, and never gam-
bles—without four aces. Chou works best when the revolutionary pendulum has swung to a point of stability. He
is a builder, not a poet.

In talks I have had with China's two great men it usually
is Chou who meticulously answers the main questions and
Mao who listens, adds a few words of caution or elucida-
tion, and enlarges the broad and dialectical view. Chou
attends countless large banquets, apparently with relish.
Mao detests feasts and prefers small groups. Chou is an
epicure but eats frugally, Mao likes simple food cooked
in the hotly seasoned Hunan style. Both men drink very
little, and each is highly disciplined in his own style. In
negotiating with President Nixon, Chou would probably
do the nitty-gritty work, in close collaboration with Mao
behind the scenes. But the final decisions would be Mao's.

Whatever the Chinese may think of Nixon's motives,
he earned some appreciation by the courtesy of coming
to see them, thereby according prestige to Mao Tse-tung
and *amour-propre* to the whole people. Vassal kings of the
past brought tributes to Peking, but never before the head

of the world's most powerful nation. The gesture in itself might go far to assuage the rancor and resentment accumulated during the past two decades. There was some risk that the gesture could be misinterpreted to the Americans' disadvantage, but more likely it would be accepted with full grace and improve chances of mutual accommodation.

The millennium seems distant and the immediate prospect is for the toughest kind of adjustment and struggle. China must satisfy Korea and Vietnam, and the U. S. cannot jettison Japan. The danger is that Americans may imagine that the Chinese are giving up communism—and Mao's world view—to become nice agrarian democrats. A more realistic world is indeed in sight. But popular illusions that it will consist of a sweet mix of ideologies, or an end to China's faith in revolutionary means, could only serve to deepen the abyss again when disillusionment occurs. A world without change by revolutions—a world in which China's closest friends would not be revolutionary states—is inconceivable to Peking. But a world of relative peace between states is as necessary to China as to America. To hope for more is to court disenchantment.

Appendixes

South of the Mountains to North of the Seas

January 9, 1965: Interview with Chairman Mao Tse-tung

After I had been back in China more than two months, I was invited to dinner by Mao Tse-tung on the night of January 9, 1965, when we conversed together for about four hours. I was the only foreign guest. Two Chinese officials present were friends from prerevolutionary days: Mme. Kung P'eng and her husband, Ch'iao Kuan-hua. I had known Kung P'eng and her sister, Kung P'u-sheng, as students at the Christian-founded Yenching University (now part of Tsing Hua University), where I briefly lectured while a resident of prewar Peking. Kung P'eng later, and for many years, was Chou En-lai's personal secretary. Now she had become Assistant to the Foreign Minister. Her husband was an Assistant Foreign Minister.[1] Both possessed a good knowledge of English.

I submitted no written questions and took no notes. I had understood that the conversations would be off the

---

[1] Kung P'eng, much lamented by her comrades and countless foreign friends, died of a brain tumor in 1970. Ch'iao Kuan-hua became chief of the first delegation of the People's Republic of China to the U.N., in November, 1971.

record, as during my visits with the Chairman in 1960. Immediately on my return home that night I wrote down everything I could recall of what had been said. The next day I was pleasantly surprised to be told that I might publish, without direct quotation, most of the dialogue. Fortunately I was able to review and correct my notes of the conversation with the help of Kung P'eng, who had kept a written record, so that this account should be substantially accurate.

Our talk ranged over what Mao himself called *shan nan hai pei,* or "from south of the mountains to north of the seas." It was *hai k'uo t'ien kung,* covering "an expanse far and wide," and in some respects unique. Mao saw countless citizens, of course, but he did not often invite non-Communist Westerners to dine with him. I believe I was the first foreigner to converse with him for publication since the People's Republic was founded, in 1949.

Why was I an exception? Probably because I had known Mao since the days when he was a hunted "Red bandit" and lived in a cave in Shensi. As a young newspaper correspondent I had made my way into Northwest China in 1936 to see what kind of men Chiang Kai-shek had been trying to "annihilate" for a decade. I was the first reporter to get into the old "Red areas" and the first to interview Mao, Chou En-lai, Lin Piao, and other leaders. Mao was then forty-three, lean, taller than the average Chinese, and toughened by the 6,000-mile retreat from South China (by way of the eastern uplands of Tibet) which is now known as the "heroic Long March." I sat in his cave for many nights while he told me his personal story and outlined a history of the Communist revolution up to that time.

Now, in his seventy-second year, a whole generation later, Mao greeted me in one of the spacious Peking-décor rooms of the magnificent Great Hall of the People, across the wide square facing T'ien An Men, the Heavenly Peace Gate of the former Forbidden City.

I had last talked to Mao in 1960, when China was in the midst of a depression caused by a cruel combination of natural and man-made disasters. Soviet technicians had been suddenly withdrawn, supplies of industrial tools cut off, and contracts for more than 300 major projects abruptly canceled. For the second consecutive year agriculture was hit by floods and drought which partly or wholly destroyed nearly half the crops. Normal production had been disrupted during experimental phases of the communes, when unattainably high goals were set for the Great Leap Forward. Mass famine was avoided only by rigidly enforced rationing. At that time Mao had told me that his people were not yet getting enough to eat. He predicted that it would take fifty years for China to catch up with the gross national product of the United States.

By January, 1965, the picture had greatly improved. Three successive good harvests had filled the national belly and some reserves of grain and meat had been accumulated. Stores everywhere displayed inexpensive basic foods and consumer goods necessities. China was paying off the last of its foreign debt to Russia, and the explosion of a nuclear device (October, 1964) had provided a new status symbol to help restore Communist—and patriotic—confidence and self-esteem.

Chairman Mao might have spoken with understandable pride of his policy of "self-reliance." He did no boasting. I found him in a philosophical mood, reflecting on his rendezvous with death and seemingly ready to leave the assessment of his own political legacy to future generations. That the old warrior had another life or two left in him, and time to launch a "Great Proletarian Cultural Revolution" to insure the lasting impact on youth of his teachings, was not to be fully revealed until the following year.

Coming at the end of several weeks of strenuous daily and nightly conferences with many provincial leaders drawn to the capital for the annual meetings of the

National People's Congress, Mao's talk with me might have been more speedily terminated had he been a sick man. He seemed wholly relaxed throughout our conversation, which began after six, continued during dinner, and went on for about two hours afterward.

One of the Chairman's doctors later told me that Mao had no organic troubles and suffered nothing beyond normal fatigue for his age. He ate moderately of a peppery Hunanese meal and drank a glass or two of Chinese grape wine, rather perfunctorily as of yore. He smoked perhaps a dozen cigarettes during the evening.

At the start of our conversation a cameraman appeared and made a short cinefilm which Mao said was done at my request. I had urged that a full recorded television interview be permitted, without much hope of success. Now I said, "Years ago I asked you to tell me your life story. You were opposed to that at first, and I argued that it would be useful to let people in China as well as abroad know what kind of person you were, and what made you work. I think you will agree that publication of your story was a good thing, not a bad thing. Now, again there are rumors that you are very ill. Wouldn't it be well to show the world, on the screen, that the rumors are greatly exaggerated?"

Mao replied, with a wry smile, that perhaps there was some doubt about that. He was soon going to see God.

Our 1960 meeting had not been reported in the Chinese press. The day of our talk in 1965 the *People's Daily* printed a large photograph of Chairman Mao and myself, in which I was identified merely as "the American author of *Red Star Over China.*" The interview in full text (only an item or two omitted, on request) is here published for the first time. In a somewhat condensed form it first appeared in *Le Nouveau Candide*, Paris, in the *Asahi*, Tokyo, February 4–14, 1965 (*et seq.*), and shortly afterward in *Stern*, Hamburg, in *L'Europeo*, Rome, in the *Sunday Times*, London, and in the *New Republic*, Washington,

D. C.[2] Minor revisions in wording (as compared to earlier publication) have been necessitated by expansion of my own notes and reconciliation of them with those of Kung P'eng.

Release of the dialogue, together with publication of a report of the meeting in the official government and Party journal, obviously lent some weight to the occasion, quite apart from a renewal of old acquaintance. It seemed to me likely that Mao wished to notify the United States, in this manner, of China's views on conditions of war and peace, especially over the question of Vietnam.

Later, on my return to China in 1970, several friends pointed out to me the possibility that the Chairman's 1960 comments, especially about going to see God, could have been intended to mislead those who were hoping to hasten him on his way. My interview as published abroad never appeared in the open press of China but I learned that it had been translated and circulated at high levels of the Party membership. Mao's flat statement that China would not intervene in Vietnam unless Chinese territory was directly attacked forecast a policy which may not have been fully endorsed at that time by the Central Committee majority headed by Liu Shao-ch'i.

Tibet and the Gods

I said: "China has been through difficult years since I last saw you but now has emerged on an impressive high level. In 1960 you told me that 90 percent of the people supported the government and only 10 percent opposed it. How does that look now?"

Mao replied that some Chiang Kai-shek elements were still around but their total was small. Many had changed their thinking and there was hope for more. As for the children of such people, they could be reeducated. Any-

[2] Major American newspapers, including the *New York Times*, declined to publish the text of this interview.

way, one could say that about 95 percent of the people, or even more, were united and supported socialism.

To myself I thought of the Panchen Lama, who had just been removed from office as acting chairman of the Preparatory Commission for the Autonomous Region of Tibet. The agrarian reform stage was being terminated and the former estates of the lama hierarchy and its stewards would soon be collectivized. After thirteen years of indoctrination of youth and landless serfs under Peking's tutelage the rapidly expanded Communist Party seemed ready to eliminate the remaining political influence of the ancient theocracy. Its authority was now thoroughly undermined by the magic of science and industry placed in the hands of the newly literate by their Maoist tutors. Lamaism and its gods were formally entering the limbo of forgotten folklore. Premier Chou En-lai had recently announced, before the National People's Congress, that the Panchen Lama was being given a "last chance to turn over a new leaf."

"Are the Panchen Lama's difficulties a matter of his feudal ties with the old lama-landlord power over the former serfs," I asked, "or would you say it was a conflict over his duties as a religious leader versus the new political power separated from the church?"

Mao replied that it was basically a matter of the land question, not religious freedom. The feudal lords had lost their land, their serfs had been freed and were now the masters. The Panchen Lama had been keeping company with some "bad eggs"[3] of the old privileged class who not only obstructed change but had organized a clique. Certain members of the clique had exposed their plans. Some people around the Panchen were not too old to reform and might yet show progress. The Panchen himself might change his ideas. He was still a member of the National People's Congress. He was now living in Peking but he

[3] *"Huai tan."*

could return to Lhasa whenever he desired; it was up to him.

As for lamaism as a religion, nobody was oppressing its true believers, all the temples were open and services maintained,[4] but the trouble was the living buddhas didn't always practice what they preached and were far from indifferent to nonspiritual affairs. The Dalai Lama himself had told Mao he didn't believe he was a living god although if one said that openly the Dalai would have to deny it. Many Christian pastors and priests also did not at all believe what they preached but many of their followers were true believers. Some people said that Mao himself had never been superstitious but that was not so. He reminded me that his mother had been a devout Buddhist and worshiped regularly; as a youth he had sided with her against his nonbelieving father. Then one day his father had walked through a lonely wood and met a tiger —a live tiger, not a paper one—and had run home as fast as possible to offer sacrifices to the gods. Wasn't that the way with many people? They prayed to the gods when in trouble but in good weather they forgot about them.

"Are there still some gods in China?"

Yes, of course; as I knew, the Chinese did not have only one god, but many. There were gods for everything: door gods, kitchen gods, rain gods, mountain gods, mercy gods, and so on. Could not even a stone become a god? There were still millions who believed in Islam and many millions more who were Buddhists and Taoists. There were also several million Christians, Catholics and Protestants. And some genuinely believed in the lama gods, too.

"I wonder if you have ever been to Tibet?"

No, he had never been to Tibet, except the eastern fringes which they crossed during the Long March. At that time he had traveled a great deal, but there were some areas he hadn't been able to see. They (the Nation-

[4] All but a few were closed during the cultural revolution.

alists) wouldn't let him see Yunnanfu (Kunming), for example. They had let him see Kweichow but they wouldn't let him see Kweiyang (the capital). Now he could probably visit Yunnan but he had not done so. He also had not been to Sinkiang (Chinese Turkestan).

Remembering that it was thirty years ago that he had first told me about his father's encounter with the tiger, he said at that time, toward the end of the first war with the Nationalists, their conditions were very poor. Yet that old Chinese Red Army was united and strong even if in numbers it was small. I had seen them when they had possessed only light weapons.

"Except for those heavy spears carried by the Poor Men's Militia."

Yes, and even broomsticks. Victory or defeat was not determined by weapons at hand at the outset. What was really decisive was the will to victory and right aims. Many elements went into that. Now more than twenty years had passed, their weapons were better, but the same factors still determined victory or defeat.

"People then were thinking mainly of liberating China from Japan. Certainly I did not then foresee the full significance of revolutionary China's rise in the world."

How the U. S. Armed Revolution

The Chairman recalled that when I had first visited him, in Pao An, they had just begun preparing for war against Japan. After reaching an agreement with Chiang Kai-shek to wage a joint war, in 1937, Mao's troops had avoided combat with the main enemy forces and concentrated on establishing guerrilla bases among the peasants. The Japanese had been of great help. They had physically occupied and burned villages over large parts of eastern China. They educated the people and quickened their political consciousness. They created conditions which made it possible for Communist-led guerrillas to increase their troops and expand their territory. Today when

Japanese came to see Mao, and apologized, he thanked them for their help. He said that he had hoped they would go as far as Sian and even Chungking. Had they done so the guerrillas' strength would have grown even more rapidly. Not only Japanese Communists but both left and right wings of the Japanese Socialists agreed that the Japanese warlords had helped the Chinese Communists.

Later on, the United States government also helped by siding with Chiang Kai-shek during the civil war. During the liberation war they had relied mainly on United States weapons turned over to them by the troops of Chiang Kai-shek. Now in Vietnam the liberation forces were being armed by the United States in the same way.

The Generalissimo had always been their teacher. Without his teaching, people like Mao himself would not have been able to rid themselves of right opportunism, and have taken up arms and fought against him. In truth it was Chiang Kai-shek and the Japanese warlords who directly taught them how to fight, while the United States had been their indirect teacher.

"Some American commentators in Saigon have compared the strength of the Vietcong there with the 1947 period in China, when the People's Liberation Army began to engage in large-scale annihilations of Nationalist forces. Are the conditions relatively comparable?"

The Chairman thought not. China's second revolutionary war had involved liberating the whole vast countryside. By 1947 the People's Liberation Army already had more than a million men, against several million troops on Chiang Kai-shek's side. The P.L.A. had then used divisional and group army strength, whereas the South Vietnamese Liberation Forces were now operating at battalion or at most regimental strength. American forces in Vietnam were still relatively small. Of course if they increased they could help speed up the arming of the people against them. But if I should tell United States leaders that they were building up a revolutionary movement which would defeat them, they would not listen. They would not let the Vietnamese decide their own affairs. Had they listened to Ngo Dinh Diem? Both Ho Chi Minh and he (Mao) thought that Ngo Dinh Diem was not so bad. They had expected the Americans to maintain him for several more years. But impatient American generals became disgusted with Diem and got rid of him. After all, following his assassination, was everything between Heaven and Earth more peaceful?

"Can Vietcong forces now win victory by their own efforts alone?"

Yes, he said, he thought that they could. Their position was relatively better than that of the Communists during the first (revolutionary) civil war (1927-37) in China. At that time there was no direct foreign intervention but now already the Vietcong had the American intervention to help arm and educate the rank and file and the army officers. Those opposed to the United States were no longer confined to the Liberation Army. Diem had not wanted to take orders. Now this independence had spread to the generals. The American teachers were succeeding.

Asked whether some of these generals would soon join the Liberation Army, Mao said yes, that some would eventually follow the example of Kuomintang generals who had turned over to the Communists.

ON THE THIRD WORLD

"United States intervention in Vietnam, the Congo, and other former colonial battlefields suggests a question of some theoretical interest as seen within Marxist concepts. The question is whether the contradiction between neo-colonialism and the revolutionary forces in what the French like to call the 'Third World'—the so-called under-developed or ex-colonial or still colonial nations of Asia, Africa, and Latin America—is today the principal political contradiction in the world? Or do you consider that the basic contradiction is still one between the capitalist countries themselves?"

Mao Tse-tung said that he had not reached an opinion about that. Perhaps I could help him? He recalled that President Kennedy had also been interested in that question. Had he not declared that as far as the United States, Canada, and Western Europe were concerned there was not much real and basic difference? The President had said that the real problem of the future was in the southern hemisphere. In advocating "Special Forces" and training to meet "local revolutionary wars" the late President might have had my question in mind.

On the other hand, contradictions between imperialists were what had caused two world wars in the past, and their struggles against colonial revolutions had not changed their character. Weren't those wars fought for the purpose of redividing colonies? If another big war occurred wouldn't it be for the purpose of redividing control over the so-called underdeveloped countries? In fact, the so-called developed countries were not so united today. If one looked at France one saw two reasons for De Gaulle's policies. The first was to assert independence from American domination. The second was to attempt to adjust French policies to changes occurring in the Asian-African countries and Latin America. The result was intensified contradiction between the imperialist nations. But was France part of its so-called "Third World"? Recently he had asked some French visitors about that and they had told him no, that France was a developed country and could not be a member of the "Third World" of undeveloped countries. It seemed that the matter was not so simple.

"Perhaps it could be said that France is in the Third World but not of it?"

Perhaps. This question which had engaged the interest of President Kennedy had led him (Mao said he had read) to study Mao's own essays on military operations. He had also learned from Algerian friends during their struggle against France that the French were reading his works and using his information against them. But at that time he had told the Algerian prime minister, Abad, that his own (Mao's) books were based on Chinese experience and would not work in reverse. They could be adapted to the waging of people's wars of liberation but were rather useless in an anti-people's war. They did not save the French from defeat in Algeria. Chiang Kai-shek had also studied the Communists' materials but he had not been saved either.

Mao remarked that the Chinese also study American books, but that it would be bad for them to fight an anti-people's war. For instance, he had read *The Uncertain Trumpet,* by General Maxwell Taylor, the United States ambassador in Saigon. General Taylor's view was that nuclear weapons probably could not be used, therefore nonnuclear arms would decide. He favored developing nuclear weapons but wanted priority in their development given to the army. Now he had his chance to test out his theories of special warfare. He had been in Vietnam only since last June, not as long as the duration of the Korean war. In Vietnam General Taylor would gain some valuable experience.

The Chairman had also read some articles of war on how to handle guerrillas issued by United States authorities to their troops. These instructions dealt with the short-comings and military weaknesses of the guerrillas and held out hopes for American victory. They ignored the decisive political fact that whether it was Diem or some other puppets, no government cut off from the masses could win against wars of liberation. No good could result from helping such governments. The Americans (authorities) would not listen to him, however. They also would not listen to me.

"In Southeast Asia as well as in India and certain countries of Africa and even Latin America there exist some social conditions comparable to those that brought on the Chinese revolution. Each country has its own problems and solutions will vary widely, yet I wonder if you agree

that social revolutions will occur which may borrow much
from the Chinese experience?"

Antifeudal and anticapitalist sentiments combined with
opposition to imperialism and neocolonialism, he replied,
grew out of oppression and wrongs of the past. Wherever the latter existed there would be revolutions but
in most countries I was talking about the people were
merely seeking national independence, not socialism—
quite another matter. European countries had also had
antifeudal revolutions, but the United States had had no
real feudal period.

"The United States had a brief period of regional
feudalism during the period of slavery in the southern
states. After a hundred years the ex-slaves are still fighting for social and political equality, so one can't say that
feudal influences don't hang on in the United States."

The United States, he said, had first fought a progressive war of independence from British imperialism, and
then fought a civil war to establish a free labor market.
Washington and Lincoln were progressive men of their
time. When the United States first established a republic
it was hated and dreaded by all the crowned heads of
Europe. That showed that the Americans were then revolutionaries. Now the American people needed to struggle
for liberation from their own monopoly capitalists. What
part of the United States did I come from?

"I was born in Missouri, the Middle West, in a geo-
graphical situation comparable to your native province,
Hunan. We have produced no revolutionaries but
Missouri produced Mark Twain and Harry Truman—two
quite different articles. Missouri was not a slave state, but
it was part of the homeland of American Indians taken
from them hardly two hundred years ago. Americans
think they are not imperialists but the American Indians
are of a different opinion. China was not quite so ruthless
in despoiling the minority peoples. After 3,000 years,
more than half the area of the country is theirs and you

still have nearly fifty million non-Han autonomous peoples. How are relations between the Han and the minority peoples today?"

He said that they were improving. In a word, the important thing was to respect them and treat them as equals.

"Among the roughly three-fifths of the earth which belongs in the Third World category very acute problems exist, as we know. The gap between the ratio of population growth and production is becoming more and more advantageous. The gap between their standard of living and that of the affluent countries is rapidly widening. Under such conditions will time wait for the Soviet Union to demonstrate the superiority of the socialist system— and then wait a century for parliamentarism to arise in the underdeveloped areas and peacefully establish socialism?"

Mao thought it would not wait so long.

"Does that question not perhaps touch upon the nexus of China's ideological dispute with the Soviet Union?"

He agreed that it did.

"Do you think it would be possible to complete not only the national liberation of emerging nations of the Third World but also their modernization, without another world war?"

Use of the word "complete" must give one pause, he said. Most of the countries concerned were still very far from socialist revolutions. In some there were no Communist parties at all while in others there were only revisionists. It was said that Latin America had about twenty Communist parties; of those eighteen had issued resolutions against China. He paused and ended by saying that only one thing was certain. Wherever severe oppression existed there would be revolution.

KHRUSHCHEV AND THE CULT

"Western commentators, and especially the Italian Communists, severely criticized the Soviet leaders for the conspiratorial and undemocratic way in which Khrushchev was thrown aside. What is your view about that?"

Mao did not directly answer the question. He replied that Mr. Khrushchev had not been very popular in China even before his fall. Few portraits of him were to be seen. But Khrushchev's books were for sale in the bookstores before the fall and they were still for sale here but not in Russia. The world needed Khrushchev; his ghost would linger on. There were bound to be people who liked him. China would miss him as a negative example.

"On the basis of your own 70/30 standards—that is, a man's work may be judged satisfactory if it is 70 percent correct and only 30 percent in error—how would you grade the present leadership of the Soviet Party? How far is it still below passing?"

Mao said he would not choose to discuss the present leaders in those terms.

"Is there any improvement in Sino-Soviet relations?"

Possibly some but not much. The chief difference was that the disappearance of Khrushchev had deprived them of a good target for polemical articles.

"In the Soviet Union," I said, "China has been criticized for fostering a 'cult of personality.' Is there a basis for that?"

Mao thought that perhaps there was some. It was said that Stalin had been the center of a cult of personality, and that Khrushchev had none at all. The Chinese people, critics said, had some feelings or practices of this kind. There might be some reasons for saying that. Probably Mr. Khrushchev fell because he had had no cult of personality at all. . . .

"While you were making a revolution in China you also revolutionized foreign Sinology and now there are various schools of Maoists and Pekingologists. Not long ago I attended a conference where professors debated whether you had or had not made any original contributions to Marxism. I asked one professor, at the close of the conference, whether it would make any difference in their controversy if it could be shown that Mao himself had never claimed to have made any creative contribution. The professor impatiently replied, 'No, indeed. That would be quite beside the point.' "

Mao laughed. More than 2000 years ago, he said, Chuang Chou wrote his immortal essays (in *The Chuang Tzu*) on the thought of Lao Tzu. A hundred schools of thought then arose to dispute the meaning of *The Chuang Tzu*.

"In 1960 when I last saw you I asked whether you ever wrote or had any intention of writing an autobiography. You replied that you had not, except as you had told me something about your life. Nevertheless, some professors have discovered 'autobiographies' written by you. A question currently exercising the professors is whether you in fact wrote your celebrated philosophical essays, 'On Contradiction' and 'On Practice' in the summer of 1937, as asserted in your *Selected Works*, or whether they were really composed some years afterward. I myself seem to recall having seen unpublished longhand translations of those essays in the summer of 1938. Would you give me your own opinion about when you composed those two essays?"

He replied that he had indeed written them in the summer of 1937. During the weeks preceding and immediately following the Lukouchiao incident[5] there had been a lull in his life in Yenan. The army had left for the front and Mao had found time to collect materials for some lectures on basic philosophy for use in the (Yenan) Anti-Japanese Academy. Some simple and yet fundamental text was needed for the young students being prepared, in brief three-month courses, for political guidance during

[5] The beginning of the major Japanese invasion of China south of the Great Wall, an event Mao had predicted; his accuracy enormously enhanced his prestige both as a Party and as a national leader.

the years immediately ahead. At the insistence of the Party Mao prepared "On Contradiction" and "On Practice" to sum up the experience of the Chinese revolution, by combining the essentials of Marxism with concrete and everyday Chinese examples. Mao said that he wrote most of the night and slept during the day. What he had written over a period of weeks he delivered in lecture form in a matter of two hours. Mao added that he himself considered "On Practice" a more important essay than "On Contradiction."

"An essay called 'Dialectical Materialism,' not included in your *Selected Works*, has been attributed to you by Mao Tse-tung specialists in the West.[6] Did you write any such essay?"

Mao asked for the question to be repeated. He replied that he had never written an essay entitled "Dialectical Materialism." He thought that he would remember it if he had.

"You were very busy learning about the art of war from 1927 onward. Had you found time to read Hegel before 1937?"

Mao said that he had read Hegel and he had also read Engels before then. He added (thinking of his American critics, perhaps) that he had never read any American Marxist theorists. Were there any good ones? I asked whether in his youth he had heard of Thorstein Veblen's *Theory of the Leisure Class*. If it had been translated into Chinese Mao had not seen it. I mentioned a book which had made a big impression on nineteenth-century American utopian socialists, and was still very interesting reading for its prophetic quality, Edward Bellamy's *Looking Backward*. As for modern American Marxist thinkers, there was Paul Sweezy's *Theory of Capitalist Development*. Mao said he regretted that he had not read any of them.

[6] See *China Quarterly*, No. 19, July-Sept., 1964, London.

THE BOMB

"Speaking of tigers, as we were," I said, "do you still believe that the bomb is a paper tiger?"

That had been just a way of talking, he said, a figure of speech. Of course the bomb could kill people. But in the end the people would destroy the bomb. Then it would truly become a paper tiger.

"You have been quoted as saying that China had less fear of the bomb than other nations because of her vast population. Other peoples might be totally wiped out but China would still have a few hundred millions left to begin anew. Was there ever any factual basis to such reports?"

He asked when and how he was supposed to have said that. I replied that one source was attributed to a Yugoslav diplomat who claimed that Mao had said that even if all Europeans were wiped out China would still have 300 millions left.

Mao answered that he had no recollection of saying anything like that but he might have said it. He did recall a conversation he had had with Jawaharlal Nehru when the latter visited China (in October, 1954). As he remembered it he had said China did not want a war. They didn't have atom bombs, but if other countries wanted to fight there would be a catastrophe in the whole world, meaning that many people would die. As for how many, nobody could know. He was not speaking only of China. He did not believe one atom bomb would destroy all mankind, so that you would not be able to find a government to negotiate peace. He had mentioned this to Nehru during their conversation. Nehru said that he was chairman of the Atomic Energy Commission of India and he knew about the destructiveness of atomic power. He was sure that no one could survive. Mao replied that it would probably not be as Nehru said. Existing governments might disappear but others would arise to replace them.

He had heard that Americans had made a film called

On the Beach, which showed nuclear war bringing the world to an end. Was that a scientific film?

"It's what is called science fiction."

Not so long ago, said Mao, Mr. Khrushchev had announced that he had a deadly weapon capable of killing all living things. Then he immediately retracted his statement—not only once but many times. Mao would not deny anything he had said, nor did he wish me to deny for him this so-called rumor (about the power of survival of China's millions in a nuclear war). Americans also had said very much about the destructiveness of the atom bomb and Khrushchev had made a big noise about that. They had all surpassed him in this respect (boasting of their destructive potency), so that he was more backward than they, was not that so?[7]

Yet recently he had reports of an investigation by Americans who visited the Bikini Islands six years after nuclear tests were conducted there. From 1959 onward research workers had been in Bikini. When they first entered the main island they had had to cut open paths through the undergrowth. They had found mice scampering about and fish swimming in the streams as usual. The well water was potable, plantation foliage was flourishing, and birds were twittering in the trees. Bacteria had multiplied at the rate of 400 kilograms per square *mou.* Probably there had been two bad years after the tests but nature had gone on. How was it that mice had survived? Plant life was destroyed but not the seeds which lay dormant until the earth's surface was purified. For the bacteria, the birds, the mice, and the trees, the atom bomb really was a paper tiger. Possibly for man himself it was different . . .

The deeper implication of Mao's last remark—and Kung P'eng later agreed with me—was that even if man

[7] Mao was ridiculing, by implication, those who supposed him to be an ignorant peasant unaware of the full meaning of nuclear terror.

disappeared from the earth—committed mass suicide—
life could not be extinguished by man's bomb.

DISARMAMENT?

All the governments were talking about complete and
total disarmament. China herself had proposed disarmament since a long time past. So had the Soviet Union.
The U.S.A. kept talking about it. What we were getting
instead was complete and thorough rearmament.

"President Johnson may find it difficult to settle problems in the East one by one. Perhaps if he desired to
expose the world to the real complexity of those problems
he might do worse than to cut to the heart of the matter
by accepting China's proposal to hold a summit conference to consider the total destruction of nuclear weapons."

Mao agreed but concluded that it would be quite
impossible. Even if Mr. Johnson himself desired such a
meeting he was after all but a bailiff[8] for the monopoly
capitalists—and they would never permit it. China had
had only one atomic explosion and perhaps it had to be
proved that one could divide into two, and so on ad
infinitum. Yet China did not want a lot of bombs, which
were really quite useless since probably no nation dared
employ them. A few would suffice for scientific experiments. Even one bomb was not liked in China's hands.

"I remember your telling me a story about an ignorant
local warlord in South China who posted a bulletin offer-
ing a reward for the capture of 'Mr. Soviet,'[9] rumored to
be leading some bandits and causing lots of trouble. Now
it is Mr. China A-Bomb that is causing trouble. Why is
that?"

[8] *Huang liang chuang t'ou*, an estate overseer.
[9] *Su-Wei-Ai*, the characters used in the phonetic transliteration of
the Russian word "Soviet," was meaningless to politically unsophis-
ticated Chinese, so the warlord's assumption that he was dealing
with a surname was quite reasonable. The Communists dropped use
of this foreign term (as an internal political aspiration) after the
Kiangsi period.

Yes, Mao feared that his reputation was not good; the imperialists just did not like him. They didn't like Mr. China A-Bomb. Yet was it really just to blame Mr. China A-Bomb for everything and to start anti-Chinese movements? Did China kill Ngo Dinh Diem? And yet that had happened. When the assassination of President Kennedy occurred the Chinese (Communists) were quite surprised. They had not planned that. Once more, they were quite surprised when Khrushchev was removed in Russia. They had not ordered that.

On the United Nations

"Indonesia has withdrawn from the United Nations, accompanied by applause from China.[10] Do you think the move will set a precedent and that other withdrawals will follow?"

Mao said that it was the United States which had first set the precedent, by excluding China from the United Nations. Now that a majority of nations might favor restoring China's seat despite U. S. opposition, there was a new scheme to require a two-thirds majority instead of a simple majority. But the question was, had China gained or lost by being outside the U.N. during the past fifteen years? Indonesia had left because she felt that there was not much advantage to remaining in the U.N. As for China, was it not in itself a United Nations? Any one of several of China's minority nationalities was much larger in population and territory than some states in the U.N. whose votes had helped deprive China of her seat there. China was a large country with plenty of work to keep her busy outside the U.N.

What did I think? Would China have been better off being in the U.N. during the past fifteen years?

"Yes, perhaps so, if it did not mean dividing one China into two Chinas. But some people now say that China does not want to join the U.N. under any conditions—?"

[10] Indonesia returned to the U.N. in 1966, after the army overthrew Sukarno and destroyed the Indonesian Communist Party.

To say that would be bad. If two-thirds of the U.N. invited China to join, and if the Chinese did not accept, wouldn't they be called nationalists? (That is, anti-internationalists.) But even if the U.N. decided to recognize mainland China rather than the Taiwan clique, wouldn't there still be difficulties? How could they give a seat to China while still condemning her as an aggressor? (Referring to the U.N. resolution which branded China an aggressor for intervening after American troops crossed into northern Korea.) But suppose the title of aggressor were even taken away from China? What then? Would the U.N. brand the U.S. an aggressor in Vietnam? Probably the United States would not agree to such changes. Thus there was no danger of China entering the U.N.

"Is it now practicable to consider forming a union of nations excluding the United States?"

Mao pointed out that such forums already existed. One example was the Afro-Asian Conference. Another was Ganefo—Games of the New Emerging Forces—organized after the United States excluded China from the Olympics.

(Preparations for the Afro-Asian Conference scheduled to open in Algiers in March, 1965, had been plagued by many problems. These included the Indonesia-Malaysia dispute and insistence on the part of the pro-China Bandung powers that the U.S.S.R. must be excluded from the Conference, as a strictly European power. China then regarded the Afro-Asian organization as the potential center of planned development of a Third World largely independent of neocolonial or Western capital. Following Chinese principles of "self-reliance" in internal development, and of mutual help between the Afro-Asian states, the process of modernization might by-pass the slow and painful methods of capital accumulation by traditional bourgeois means. Such a theoretical alternative of course would have implied more rapid and radical political evolution and an earlier arrival at presocialist conditions in the capital-poor Afro-Asian states. It had been obvious for some time that the Afro-Asian Conference was also viewed as a potential permanent assembly of the have-not nations to exist independently from the American-dominated United Nations from which China and her closest allies had long been excluded and from which Indonesia had recently excluded itself. Events moved in a different direction, to a great extent helped by Sino-Soviet hostility.)

HOW MANY CHINESE?

"In fact, Mr. Chairman, how many people are there inside China's own United Nations," I asked. "Can you give me a population figure resulting from the recent census?"[11]

The Chairman replied that he really did not know. Some said that there were 680 to 690 millions but he did not believe it. How could there be so many?

When I suggested that it ought not to be difficult to calculate, on the basis of ration coupons (cotton and rice) alone, Mao indicated that the peasants had sometimes confused the picture. Before Liberation they had hidden births and kept sons off the register out of fear of having them conscripted. Since Liberation there had been a tendency to report greater numbers and less land, and to minimize output returns while exaggerating the effects of calamities. Nowadays a new birth was reported at once, but when someone died it might not be reported for months. (His implication seemed to be that extra ration coupons could be accumulated in that way.) No doubt there had been a real decline in the birth rate, but the peasants were still too slow to adopt family planning and birth control. The decline in the death rate was probably greater than the decline in births. Average longevity had gone up from about thirty years to close to fifty years.

THE U. S. IN VIETNAM

"Do you have any advice for the U.S.A.?"

They had already suggested, a long time ago, that the

[11] A sampling census was held in the spring and summer of 1964 but no official results were announced.

United States withdraw a bit. The United States had its hands stretched all over the world. As usual, the American rulers would not listen.

The American position was difficult, especially in Vietnam. To withdraw was not good; not to withdraw was also not good.[12] Wherever there were signs of disturbance the American imperialists must send troops, first moving here and then there.

"I have heard some people in Washington argue that the fleet and the marines might as well be in Vietnam as anywhere else. They have to be paid anyway."

Yes, they had plenty to do. Reactionaries everywhere needed their help. In the Congo, for instance. In the end, they must all go home. In the past China had seen American troops in Tientsin, Tsingtao, Shanghai, even Peking. They had all left. In fact they had left very rapidly.

The conditions of revolutionary anti-imperialist victory in China had been, first, that the old ruling group was weak and incompetent, led by Chiang Kai-shek, a man who was always losing battles. Second, the People's Liberation Army was strong and ably led and people believed in its cause. In places where such conditions did not prevail the Americans could intervene. Otherwise they would stay away or soon leave.

We were at dinner when Mao asked whether I considered that Mr. Johnson *could* try a Vietnam policy any different from that of his predecessors. I said probably not; it would be easier to follow the old ruts deeper into the trap. But the war in Vietnam was not popular and Mr. Johnson liked to be popular. His administration faced many internal problems which a bigger war in Asia could not really solve. In balance, however, since Ho Chi Minh and Mao Tse-tung probably would not provide Mr. Johnson with "an attractive way out," he would not leave until the costs became very great. I had already

[12] *Pu-hao . . . yeh pu-hao.*

given my opinion to Foreign Minister Ch'en Yi, that "it would not surprise me to see 100,000 American troops in Vietnam before next year."

Mao asked what kind of internal problems Mr. Johnson faced.

I ticked off several obvious ones, including unemployment, especially high among blacks, which helped to increase racial tension. War could, of course, tend to cut down unemployment temporarily. Automation was a factor in unemployment, and I also mentioned the great population shift from the farms, where mechanization and capitalization had eliminated so many small proprietors and poured millions of landless people into the urban labor market. Now only about 8 percent of the total U. S. population was needed to produce more food than the country could consume.

Mao asked me to repeat the figure. When I did so he shook his head skeptically. How could that be? was all he said.

China and the U. S.

"Naturally I personally regret that forces of history have divided and separated the American and Chinese peoples from virtually all communication during the past fifteen years. Today the gulf seems broader than ever. However, I myself do not believe it will end in war and one of history's major tragedies."

Mao said that forces of history were also bound, eventually, to bring the two peoples together again; that day would surely come. Possibly I was right that meanwhile war could be avoided.

War could occur only if American troops came to China. They might come and they might not come. If they came they would not really benefit much. That simply would not be allowed. Probably the American leaders knew that and consequently they would not invade China. *Then there would be no war because if they did not send troops to China the Chinese certainly would never send troops to attack the United States.*

"What of the possibilities of war arising over Vietnam? I have read many newspaper stories indicating that the United States has considered expanding the war into North Vietnam."

No, that would not happen. Mr. Rusk had now made it clear that the U. S. would not do that. Mr. Rusk might have earlier said something like that but now he had corrected himself and said that he had never made such a statement. Therefore, there need not be any war in North Vietnam.

"Judging from conversations I have had from time to time with a few high American officials, including Dean Rusk, I would say that the makers and administrators of United States policy, the rulers of the United States, simply do not understand you."

Why not? *China's armies would not go beyond her borders to fight. That was clear enough. Only if the United States attacked China would the Chinese fight. Wasn't that clear? Chinese were very busy with their internal affairs. Fighting beyond one's own borders was criminal. Why should the Chinese do so? The South Vietnamese could cope with their situation.*

"American officials repeatedly say that if United States forces were withdrawn from Vietnam then all Southeast Asia would be overrun."

The question is, said Mao, "overrun" by whom? Overrun by Chinese or overrun by the inhabitants? China was overrun but only by Chinese.

"Are there now any Chinese troops in Vietnam?"

Mao affirmed that there were no Chinese forces in northern Vietnam or anywhere else in Southeast Asia. *China had no troops outside her own frontiers.*

"Dean Rusk has said that if China would give up her aggressive policies then the United States would withdraw from Vietnam. What does he mean?"

Mao replied that China had no policies of aggression to abandon. Where was China aggressing? China had committed no acts of aggression. China supported revolutionary movements, but not by invading countries. Of course, whenever a liberation struggle existed China would publish statements and call demonstrations to support it. It was precisely that which vexed the imperialists.

Mao went on to say that on some occasions China deliberately made a loud noise, as, for example, around Quemoy and Matsu. A flurry of shots there could attract a lot of attention perhaps because the Americans were uneasy so far away from home. Consider what could be accomplished by firing some blank shells within those Chinese territorial waters. Not so long ago the United States Seventh Fleet in the Taiwan Straits was deemed insufficient to reply to the shells. The U.S. also dispatched part of its Sixth Fleet in China's direction and brought over part of the navy from San Francisco. Arrived here, they had found nothing to do. So it seemed that China could order the American forces to march here or to march there.

It was the same with Chiang Kai-shek's army. They had been able to order Chiang to scurry this way and then to hurry off in another direction. Of course when navy men were warm and had full bellies they must be given something to do. But how was it that shooting off empty guns at home could be called aggression while those who actually intervened with arms and bombed and burned people of other lands were not considered aggressors?

Some Americans had once said that the Chinese revolution was led by Russian aggressors but in truth the Chinese revolution was armed by Americans. In the same way the Vietnamese revolution was also being armed by Americans, not by China. The liberation forces had not only greatly improved their supplies of American weapons during recent months but had also expanded their forces by recruiting American-trained troops and officers from the puppet armies of South Vietnam. China's liberation forces had grown in numbers and strength by recruiting to their side the troops trained and armed by the Americans for Chiang Kai-shek. The movement was called the "changing of hats." When Nationalist soldiers changed hats in large numbers because they had no confidence in their officers and felt that they would be killed needlessly, that the peasants would kill them for wearing the wrong hat, then the end was near. Changing hats was becoming more popular now among the Vietnamese puppets.

"Do you mean to say that the circumstances of victory for the Liberation Front now exist in South Vietnam?"

Mao thought that the American forces were not yet ready to leave. Fighting would go on perhaps for one to two years. After that the United States troops would find it uninteresting and might go home or go somewhere else.

"In a recent interview with Premier Chou En-lai, I understood him to say that China would oppose a Geneva Conference to enforce the Treaty of 1954 unless the United States first withdrew its troops from Vietnam. Is it your policy now to insist upon the withdrawal of United States forces before participating in a Geneva Conference to discuss the international position of a unified Vietnam?"

The Chairman said that he did not know what Premier Chou had said to me. *He himself thought that several possibilities should be mentioned. First, a conference might be held and United States withdrawal would follow. Second, the conference might be deferred until after the withdrawal. Third, a conference might be held but United States troops might stay around Saigon, as in the case of South Korea. Finally, the South Vietnamese Front might drive out the Americans without any conference or international agreement.*

The 1954 Geneva Conference had provided for the withdrawal of French troops from all Indochina and had forbidden any intervention by any other foreign troops.

The United States had nevertheless violated the Geneva convention and that could happen again. . . . Frankly, it was a good thing for the United States to keep troops in South Vietnam. That trained the people and made their Liberation Army strong. It was not enough to have a single Ngo Dinh Diem, just as in China a single Chiang Kai-shek had not been enough. There had to be a Japan to overrun the country for eight and a half years. Only then did the nation develop able leaders and a strong revolutionary army able to defeat the internal reactionaries and drive out the American imperialists.

"How would China respond if the United States adopted a peace policy, offered to withdraw its forces from South Korea, Taiwan, all Southeast Asia, everywhere abroad, if China and other powers would agree not only to total destruction of nuclear weapons but to total world disarmament?"

Mao said that frankly he had never given any thought to such a notion.

"I have never met President Johnson, but I suppose that if you had any special message for him I might be able to give it to him. Is there anything you would like to say to him?"

After a pause: No, there was not.[13]

"Under the circumstances," I asked, "do you really see any hope of an improvement in Sino-American relations?"

Yes, he thought there was hope. It would take time. Maybe there would be no improvement in his generation (lifetime). He was soon going to see God.[14]

GOING TO SEE GOD

"Speaking of your health, as we were not, judging from this evening you seem to be in good condition."

[13] Simply, *Pu-shih!*

[14] In Chinese, *"Pu chiu yao chien Shang-ti,"* "to be obliged to see God before long." Mao used *Shang-ti*, meaning the "Emperor God," supreme over all other gods, a term less ambiguous than *T'ien*, which can mean God as Nature or a universal primordial principle.

Mao Tse-tung smiled wryly and replied that there was perhaps some doubt about that. He said again that he was getting ready to see God very soon. Did I believe it?

"I wonder if you mean you are going to find out whether there is a God. Do you believe *that*?"

No, he did not, but some people who claimed to be well informed said that there was a God. There seemed to be many gods and sometimes the same god could take all sides. In the wars of Europe the Christian God had been on the side of the British, the French, the Germans, and so on, even when they were fighting each other. At the time of the Suez Canal crisis God was united behind the British and the French but then there was Allah to back up the other side.

At dinner Mao had mentioned that both his brothers had been killed. His first wife had also been executed during the revolution (1930) and their son had been killed during the Korean war. Now, he said that it was odd that death had so far passed him by. He had been prepared for it many times but death just did not seem to want him. What could he do? On several occasions it had seemed that he would die. His personal bodyguard was killed while standing right beside him. Once he was splashed all over with the blood of another soldier but the bomb had not touched him.

"Was that in Yenan?"

In Yenan, too. His bodyguard had been killed during the Long March.[15] There had been other narrow escapes. According to laws of dialectics all struggles must finally be resolved, including man's struggle for life on this earth.

"Accidents of fate which spared you have made possible perhaps the most remarkable career in Chinese history. In all China's long annals I cannot recall any man who rose from rural obscurity not only to lead a successful

[15] In 1935 Mao's brother Mao Tse-t'an was also killed in combat. The youngest brother, Mao Tse-min, made the Long March and was killed in 1942, in an anti-Communist purge in Sinkiang.

social revolution but to write its history, to conceive the strategy of its military victory, to formulate an ideological doctrine which changed the traditional thought of China, and then to live out the practice of his philosophy in a new kind of civilization with broad implications for the whole world."

After a moment of reflection Mao said that I knew he had begun life as a primary school teacher. He had then had no thought of fighting wars. Neither had he thought of becoming a Communist. He was more or less a democratic personage such as myself. Later on—he sometimes wondered by what chance combination of reasons—he had become interested in founding the Chinese Communist Party. Anyway, events did not move in accordance with the individual will. What mattered was that China had been oppressed by imperialism, feudalism, and bureaucratic capitalism. Such were the facts. . . .

"Youths who heard you lecture in 1937 later learned about revolution in practice, but what can be the substitute for youths in China today?"

Of course those in China now under the age of twenty had never fought a war and never seen an imperialist or known capitalism in power. They knew nothing about the old society at first hand. Parents could tell them but to hear about history and to read books was not the same thing as living it.

"Man makes his own history but he makes it in accordance with his environment. You have fundamentally changed the environment in China. Many wonder what the younger generation bred under easier conditions will do. What do you think about it?"

He also could not know, he said. He doubted that anyone could be sure. There were two possibilities. There could be a continued development of the revolution toward communism. The other possibility was that youth could negate the revolution and do bad things (*kan huai shih*): make peace with imperialism, bring the remnants of the Chiang Kai-shek clique back to the mainland, and take a stand beside the small percentage of counterrevolutionaries still in the country. I had asked his opinion. Of course he did not hope for counterrevolution but future events would be decided by future generations, and in accordance with conditions we could not foresee. From the long-range view future generations ought to be more knowledgeable than we are, just as men of the bourgeois-democratic era were more knowledgeable than those of the feudal ages. Their judgment would prevail, not ours. The youth of today and those to come after them would assess the work of the revolution in accordance with values of their own.

Mao's voice dropped away and he half closed his eyes. Man's condition on this earth was changing with ever increasing rapidity. A thousand years from now all of us, he said, even Marx, Engels, and Lenin, would probably appear rather ridiculous.

Before I rose to leave the Chairman sent his greetings to the American people and said simply that he wished them progress. If he wished them liberation weren't some people bound to disagree? Wouldn't they say that they already had the right to vote? But to those among them who were not really liberated, and desired liberation, to them he wished his best.

Mao Tse-tung walked me through the doorway and, despite my protests, saw me to my car, where he stood alone for a moment, coatless in the subzero Peking night, to wave me farewell in the traditional manner of that ancient cultured city. I saw no security guards around the entrance nor can I now recall having seen even one armed bodyguard in our vicinity all evening. Two or three simply dressed young women had been in and out of the room, sometimes standing in the background, as if orderlies. Could they have been Mao's daughters? One held his arm as he stood up.

Mao shook hands and gave me a precautionary word,

to take care, quoting a Chinese maxim: "Unpredictable high winds and misfortunes are in the skies!"

As the car drove away I looked back and watched Mao brace his shoulders and slowly retrace his steps and reenter the Great Hall of the People.

Talks with Chou En-lai, 1964

October 22, December 16, 1964: Interviews with
Premier Chou En-lai

In two interviews with Premier Chou En-lai I was given some facts and estimates on 1964 Chinese agricultural and industrial production which were the first information of the kind officially made available for four years. They suggested that China had attained some gratifying levels in food output and in selected lines of industry, and that the people had about recovered from the 1959-61 setbacks of successive crop failures combined with total withdrawal of Soviet aid. The Premier cautiously avoided any overstatement, in line with a general view here that China needed another year or two of bumper harvests in order to assure a safe passage across the threshold into relative plenty.

Chou En-lai received me twice in his residence inside the official quarters within the former Forbidden City and our talks lasted about four hours. He looked very fit and laughed at rumors concerning his "serious illness." Despite his sixty-six years his hair showed few streaks of gray. The earthy realism of some of his remarks carried strong implications of dislike for adventurism or gambling coupled with a profound awareness of the decades of work, stretching far beyond his own time, required to make China a fully modernized nation. Some of his talk was off the record but he agreed to paraphrasing in most instances and direct quotations in others.

In his survey of foreign relations the Premier offered no hope of any immediate easing of Sino-American tension. He said that (possible) recognition of an "independent" Taiwan government would make that impossible for many years to come. If the United Nations did likewise China would reject any future contact with that body. He applauded General de Gaulle for "saving" France and especially for his fiscal policy of independence. In ten major points of dispute with Khrushchev's Russia he saw one change for the better: Khrushchev's removal. China was adamantly opposed to Soviet representation at the forthcoming Afro-Asian Conference and equally opposed to an international meeting of Communist parties for which the new U.S.S.R. leaders had renewed Khrushchev's call.

Premier Chou said that preliminary reports on China's 1964 grain harvest were still about 10 percent incomplete at the end of the year but he conservatively put the total crop weight at about 200 million tons. That figure was based, he said, on actual commune sales and tax payments to the government. Other estimates, averaging out results obtained by the "sampling method" (measuring typical yields under varied conditions), were preferred by the statisticians, according to the Premier. "Sampling" estimates showed an increase of 14 to 15 percent over the 1963 harvest. (On that basis the 1964 harvest would be about 210 million tons—perhaps the highest in history— but Chinese officials cautiously avoided such maximum claims while awaiting final returns.)

The 1964 cotton harvest over large areas showed an increase of 40 to 50 percent, the Premier said. (He provided no all-area estimate. There is reason to believe that the overall average increase over 1963 was not less than 15 percent and set a new record.)

Extended irrigation works and rural electrification, increased use of chemical fertilizer, and generally favorable weather were given as reasons for agricultural recovery. (In a separate interview with the vice-minister of agriculture, Mr. Wu Chen, I was told that China's 1964 chemical fertilizer output rose to seven million tons. That was about double the figure advanced by foreign analysts in Hongkong.)

Quantitative production in steel was "still a bit below past highs" but there was an overall increase of 20 percent compared to 1963. The Premier asserted that greatly improved quality and variety in most industrial products gave China a more balanced and modern industrial economy. ("Back-yard" or native-hearth steel and iron output helped to inflate past figures. Those methods had now been largely abandoned. Foreign observers in Peking estimated 1964 modern steel production at between thirteen and fifteen million tons.)

In some old and new fields quantitative as well as qualitative gains were made. The Premier cited petroleum, in which China had currently attained "self-sufficiency," chiefly derived from bonanza strikes in the new Taching oil fields. He forecast a 1965 petroleum output of ten million tons. China now makes many types of modern fuels. In answer to my question whether I was correct in reporting, as early as 1962, that China was producing her own jet engines and jet aircraft, the Premier confirmed that such was the case. During the last few years the quality had much improved, he said.

As part of his government's dedication to raising the standard of living of the people, the Premier stressed, systematic and widespread efforts were now being made to popularize family planning or birth control. A propaganda program was being intensified but was only gradually penetrating the rural areas. (All modern and practical means of birth control were being advocated and applied—including abortion on demand.) The

Premier defined China's goal as a gradual reduction in the rate of population increase, with a target as low as that of Japan.

In the nuclear field, China would explode "nothing like the hundreds of bombs tested in the United States," which Premier Chou considered quite unnecessary. Nevertheless, China's future development of nuclear weapons— presumably the hydrogen bomb—would be "at a rate not slower than that of the industrially advanced countries." The Premier said that China's unilateral pledge not to be the first to use nuclear bombs definitely precluded use of small-yield or tactical nuclear weapons. Meanwhile, China would persist in her demand for total destruction of all nuclear weapons.

Peking's view on a solution of the South Vietnam question was to implement the 1954 Geneva Agreement for a peaceful and unified Vietnam. The Premier emphasized that the first and foremost problem was to secure the withdrawal of U. S. troops from South Vietnam, "so that the people there may resolve their internal problems by themselves."

Chou En-lai denied that border disputes were the main cause of Sino-Soviet differences. He conceded, however, that ideological differences did indeed affect the policies in many fields. He expressed deep satisfaction that by early 1965 China would have entirely liquidated its debts to the Soviet Union. Henceforth China would acquire no foreign debts. China's internal bonds would also be redeemed before 1968. (Formerly China's trade with the Soviet bloc absorbed 80 percent of her foreign commerce but in 1964 China had traded with 125 countries and regions, and over 70 percent of her foreign trade was outside the U.S.S.R.)

Our interviews began with questions concerning agriculture. Following discussion of the harvest I asked why, since the news was good, China continued to buy grain abroad. The Premier explained that such purchases two or three years ago were to alleviate real shortages but that purchases at present were of a commercial and manipulative nature. China benefited by selling rice to "many countries"—Ceylon, Cuba, and Indonesia, for example—and importing low-cost wheat to replace it for consumption in China. The wheat was sold largely in the cities, which enabled the communes to retain more of their rice for reserves in the interior. That policy would continue.

A point in dispute abroad was the extent to which "recovery" had been spurred by the extension of private plots as incentive. I asked about reports that as much as 20 percent of the total output came from that source. The Premier said that private plots were no more than 7 percent of total cultivated land and would not be permitted to increase beyond 10 percent. It was hard to know the total product of the private plots. Often it went unreported but it was part of 10 percent which the statisticians' "sampling" methods indicated had been omitted from state calculations for the 1964 crop. Many private plots doubtless did give a better yield than the collective land. The peasants paid close attention to them in spare time and generously used the manure from their pigs and other sources to increase yields.

The conversation continued:

Question: "On average, is more fertilizer used on private plots than on collective acreage?"

Premier Chou: "Peasants will sell a portion of their pig manure to the collective in order to get some cash. But they generally reserve some for their own use [on private plots].

"We have a play on now entitled *Sending Manure to the Field*. It is not possible that everyone behaves like the advanced commune members depicted in the play. Otherwise, there would have been no need to stage the play. Those with penetrating eyes know that what a play calls for [in social attitudes] are precisely those things which some people still find hard to do. The play is staging something exemplary to help the less advanced catch up. Hence there is no need for Western newsmen to make any comments. We ourselves admit that not all things are advanced. We commend the advanced in order to set examples for others to follow.

"Those who come to China for fact-finding don't have to hunt for any inside information. They can discover our problems from the stage or from our publications. Of course sometimes what is advocated on the stage or in our publications may be wrong, but the general trend can be discerned. When we encourage the good and criticize the bad, it means that bad things surely still exist and good ones are not yet perfect. If everything becomes good, we will certainly look for still better things as examples.

"For instance, we are now giving publicity to the example of the Ta Chai Production Brigade. This brigade is in the Taihang Mountain area [in Shansi province] and in a place which entirely consists of sloping land where gullies are found everywhere and where the soil used to be lean and barren. But precisely in such a place people have, solely through self-reliant efforts in a decade and more, turned the entire sloping land into terraced fields, developed production, and transformed the poor valley into a rich valley.

"During the past eleven years this place borrowed money from the state only once, and repaid it the following year. It had been developed entirely through self-reliance. It is true that some big water conservancy projects are being developed [in Shansi] but those in Ta Chai were entirely built by the inhabitants. For the past eleven years each household in Ta Chai had on an average sold an annual amount of one metric ton of grain to the state [through the collective]. That is really something wonderful. The amount sold this year even greatly surpassed that figure. Ta Chai is of course quite a good example and such examples can be found in all provinces of China. China has a total rural population of more than 120 million households. If the amount of grain sold to the states by each commune or production brigade [all over China] all at once reached an average of one metric ton per household the total would be well over 120 million metric tons. This of course cannot be realized yet but it is necessary for us to promote the spirit of Ta Chai, and there is indeed the possibility for that in the future."

Communes were said to retain about 60 percent of their grain output after payment of taxes, and obligatory sales to the state. Grain deliveries of 120 million tons to the state would imply a total harvest in excess of 300 million tons—and place China in the fore among the world's grain exporters. Ta Chai in 1964 had 83 households and a total brigade population of 360, an average of 4.3 persons per household. For demographers these figures might be intriguing materials for speculation concerning the elusive "total population" figure for China, and the unrevealed results of the 1964 census.

Question: "According to China's Fifteen-Year Plan [of 1957] China would catch up with Britain in industrial production by 1973. Why does one not hear the slogan these days?"

Premier: "The overtaking of Britain is no longer the center of our attention. In 1957, when the Soviet Union set itself the goal of surpassing the United States in gross output, we raised as a goal the slogan of overtaking Britain. After we gained a whole set of experience in construction through these years of probing along the road of self-reliance, we came to realize that this should not be our main target. The modernization of our industry cannot be realized merely through the quantitative increase of a few items of industrial products. Take petroleum as an example. Britain produces practically no petroleum, and so it could be surpassed by us at one stroke if figures in this respect were taken as an index. But that would be a very low aim, and how could we say

that in so doing we had overtaken and surpassed Britain?
Now let us look at what would be for us a high aim. Take
electricity, for example. After a span of several centuries
Britain has become a modern industrialized country where
electricity is in widespread use. It has become a necessity
not only for industry but also for the ordinary consumer.
No matter what crises may occur in Britain's capitalist
economy—during which the output of steel and coal may
decrease—the output of electricity would not drop substantially because the costs of production could be met by
proceeds from the consumers. [Constant demand for non-
industrial consumption guarantees a minimum basic market.] Electric power in rural China in 1964 was twenty-two
times greater than in 1957, but it would take China quite
a long time to overtake Britain in the per capita output
of electricity. Owing to different circumstances in different countries, [there is a difference in] the amount of
specified industrial products needed by each country,
with one needing more of this and another country needing more of that. Ours is a planned economy, while theirs
is a capitalist economy. They are different in nature. The
important thing is to study the level of our industry and
technology as a whole."

Question: "Can you give me your current estimate of
China's total population? I have seen and heard convincing evidence that China's family planning system now
earnestly seeks to limit population growth. When do
you expect the annual population increase to fall below
2 percent?"

Premier: "Family planning is the first step toward our
goal. It is going on well in some cities, but this work
cannot be expected to yield immediate major results in
the countryside. The mortality is falling at a greater speed
than the birth rate. The aged are living longer and the
infant mortality is still lower. This is because the minimum means of livelihood available to the people have
improved. Of course, we cannot say that the Chinese
people are already well-to-do. But as you know very well,

their conditions are much better as compared with old China. The present standard of living in China is of course much lower than that of the United States. But we do not have five million unemployed. The life of the unemployed families in the United States is very bitter, while some others there enjoy a much higher living standard than the Chinese. In China there is no great difference between the living standards of different people, and that is why the mortality is low.

"We encourage family planning. Work in this respect has brought about fairly good results in the cities, particularly in the schools, factories, and government organs where the young people realize the advantages of late marriage and are willing to practice family planning after marriage. Family planning is practicable, but it requires proper publicity and education and it takes time. It would be indeed very satisfactory if the net increase of China's population could drop to below 1 percent within this century."

Question: "Do you see any possibility of improvement in Sino-American relations? Do you think it would be useful to have some exchange of scientists and scholars?"

Premier: "In order to improve Sino-American relations, we must start with matters of principle, and not with side issues. At the Sino-American ambassadorial talks in Warsaw, we always put forward the following two points. One is that agreement should be reached between China and the United States on peaceful coexistence on the basis of the [Bandung] Five Principles. The other is that the U. S. must withdraw all its armed forces from Taiwan and the Taiwan Straits. Once agreement can be reached on those two points of principle, other questions will be settled rather easily. Otherwise, the mere tackling of side issues will not solve the fundamental problem.

"The Warsaw talks have already been going on for more than nine years, but the United States has all along refused to agree on these two points of principle. The United States follows others in saying that it, too, is for

peaceful coexistence; but when China calls for it, the
United States refuses. Does this not prove the hypocrisy
of the words of the U. S. government? As for the question
of visits to China by some individuals, no agreement is
possible at the present time either. Those whom we welcome the U. S. government won't allow to come, while
those it wants to send to China are not welcomed by us.
In a word, when questions of principle are not settled,
there is deadlock even on minor issues. Perhaps you are
an exception. We welcome you, and the U. S. State
Department recently permitted you to come."

I interpolated a question concerning the effects on
China–United States relations of a mooted plan to create
an "independent Taiwan Republic."

"At the present time the Chiang Kai-shek clique on Taiwan claims to represent China. Of course no patriotic Chinese can agree to that. But if there should be someone on
Taiwan who is so depraved as to completely follow the
beck and call of the United States and serve the needs of
U. S. policy by declaring Taiwan an independent political
unit, and, relying on the majority in the United Nations
under the manipulation and coercion of the U. S. government, continue to usurp China's lawful seat in the United
Nations, I can tell you frankly that not only would it be
impossible to improve and to restore Sino-American relations, but, what is more, we would have nothing to do
with the United Nations. If such a situation should arise,
the Sino-American confrontation would not be a question
of a few years, it would be of a long duration of we don't
know how many years. It will remain that way until the
day comes—and I believe the day will come—when the
United States finds itself no longer able to continue along
this path and gives up this policy."

Question: "The Sato government of Japan also appears
prepared to support an American alternative plan for an
independent Taiwan. Do you consider that this is a price
Mr. Sato may be ready to pay for the return of Okinawa?"

Premier: "There is no direct connection between the

two questions. If Japan had the ability to recover Okinawa, its ideas would be different from those of the United States. Such a Japan would no longer be the Japan of today. At present it is following the U. S. government in clamoring for 'two Chinas' or 'one China, one Taiwan,' or recognizing only Taiwan. This is tailing after the U. S. policies and beating the drum for them, and this shows that Japan has neither the will nor the ability to recover Okinawa."

Question: "China advocates calling a conference of the signatories of the Geneva Agreement of 1954 to bring an end to the war in South Vietnam. Would China and the Democratic Republic of Vietnam be prepared to discuss General de Gaulle's proposal for international guarantees for the independence and neutralization of Vietnam?"

Premier: "We maintain that a peaceful and unified Vietnam should be realized in pursuance of the provisions of the 1954 Geneva Agreement and that its system should be determined according to the wishes of its people. The question of South Vietnam today is not the question of immediate calling for a conference. What is first and foremost is that American troops must be withdrawn from South Vietnam so that the South Vietnamese people may resolve their internal problems by themselves. As for the questions of respecting the peace, neutrality, and independence of Laos and Cambodia, the Geneva Conference should be called immediately to discuss them."

Question: "Judging from reports published abroad, China's bomb was of a much more 'sophisticated' nature than American experts anticipated. Just what does that mean?"

Premier: "American experts concluded from the data they collected that the technical level of the atom bomb we exploded is higher than that of the first nuclear tests of the United States, Britain, and France. On this matter the American experts know more than you do and perhaps also more than I do. Neither of us is an expert."

Question: "The increased piling up of nuclear weapons would seem as childish as boys' games with wooden soldiers, since the weapons cannot really be used. And yet each time threats are hurled down about them it is rather more like another pull on the trigger in a game of Russian roulette. Then it looks exceedingly dangerous, does it not?"

Premier: "It is not so dangerous. Why are you so afraid? Almost twenty years have passed since the Second World War."

Question: "The interval between the first and second wars was also twenty years."

Premier: "We are not fatalists. We see things from a dialectical viewpoint. A number of countries having come into possession of nuclear weapons, none now dares to risk using them. Otherwise why should [General Maxwell] Taylor have invented 'special warfare'? The interesting thing is that he is now making experiments with his invention. Our Chinese cadres [periodically] go down to basic-level units in the countryside to gather first-hand experience, and now Taylor is doing likewise [in Vietnam]. But for him it is a bitter place to go."

The Premier spoke at some length about the successes of guerrilla warfare in Vietnam and then went on to mention the rise of France since it had left Vietnam and Algeria and become a power capable of challenging the United States dollar. He continued:

"Why can De Gaulle be so proud? Because he stopped the colonial war in Algeria. In so doing he superficially seemed to have lost face by withdrawing 800,000 troops and one million civilians and recognizing the complete independence of Algeria, but actually he saved France in an economic crisis. Would it be possible for the United States to produce a president who would withdraw all U. S. troops stationed all over the world and thereby completely change the world conception of the United States?'"

Speaking of the future and the yet heavy tasks ahead, the Premier cited dramatic contrasts in the economy— the coexistence of China's giant hydraulic steel press of 16,000-tons capacity, the peer of any in the world, with transport dependent on rubber-tired carts, and of fine precision instruments and large diesel-driven ships with the peasants' sampans and their vegetable-oil lamps. It would "still take quite some time for China to become a modernized country." He concluded:

"In Shanghai, the boats for collecting and transporting fertilizers are particularly shabby. In northern Kiangsu, even more backward phenomena can be found. For instance, in Chitung county along the coast, which is situated to the southeast of Nantung, where practically all the lands are irrigated fields, there are not even any oxen, let alone agricultural machines. Why? There is no need. Each peasant has only a *mou* or more of land. And the yield is high: the output of ginned cotton is over 50 kilograms per *mou* and that of grain about 500 kilograms per *mou*. Practically all the lands are water-soaked and can be worked on by manual labor only. No deep-plowing is necessary. There is a dense network of rivers and canals in the area where the manure is carried in very small boats or by people with shoulder poles. But the yield is high and the people there are rather well off. How will mechanization be realized in those places? This remains a subject for further study.

"Conditions in China are very complicated. Take revolutionary wars, for instance; we learned quite a lot, and we did defeat Chiang Kai-shek and fight the United States. That is not mere make-believe, we shed blood for it. But frankly speaking, as the Premier I have not fully mastered China's economic construction which has been carried on for fifteen years. I have learned something, but not very well. We are all learning. The laws governing economic development are extremely complicated. We have gained some experience, but we have to acquire much more experience. We have understood some of the laws, but there are many more laws governing economic development which remain to be understood. We have done quite a few things right in the past fifteen years, but we have also done some wrong things. One must acquire both positive and negative experience. This was the case with past wars. Sometimes we won a battle and sometimes we lost it, and more than once; only then did we enrich our experience and lead our revolution to victory. The same is true of construction. In our view, only when we dare to face up to difficulties can we overcome them, and only when we dare to admit our shortcomings and mistakes can we rectify them. In this way we'll continuously march forward by ceaselessly overcoming difficulties and rectifying shortcomings and mistakes.

"Those who are not familiar with such things may think that we have been doing everything perfectly all along. How can things be so? Other types of people are bent on finding fault. When they found some shortcomings on our part, they thought that China was in extreme economic difficulties. Now that the economic situation in China has changed for the better, some people are saying that everything is wonderful. They always fail to form a correct picture about China. As far as we are concerned, we have found the right road. And while marching along this road, difficulties and shortcomings will continue to crop up, and we have to work continuously to overcome them so as to go forward, and we also have to sum up the experience and lessons continuously so as to find better methods for advancing our cause. The same is true both of revolutionary struggles and of production and construction. In other words, this is true of class struggle as well as the struggle for production. Man constantly sums up experience from practice, continues to make discoveries and inventions, and keeps on creating and advancing."

Resolutions of the Eleventh Plenum of the Central Committee of the C.C.P.— The Sixteen-Point Program of the Cultural Revolution, 1966

1. The Great Proletarian Cultural Revolution now unfolding is a great revolution that touches people to their very souls and constitutes a new stage in the development of the socialist revolution in our country, a deeper and more extensive stage.

At the Tenth Plenary Session of the Eighth Central Committee of the Party, Comrade Mao Tse-tung said: To overthrow a political power, it is always necessary, first of all, to create public opinion, to do work in the ideological sphere. This is true for the revolutionary class as well as for the counterrevolutionary class. This thesis of Comrade Mao Tse-tung's has been proved entirely correct in practice.

Although the bourgeoisie has been overthrown, it is still trying to use the old ideas, culture, customs, and habits of the exploiting classes to corrupt the masses, capture their minds, and endeavor to stage a comeback. The proletariat must do just the opposite: it must meet head-on every challenge of the bourgeoisie in the ideological field and use the new ideas, culture, customs, and habits of the proletariat to change the mental outlook of the whole of society. At present, our objective is to struggle against and crush those persons in authority who are taking the capitalist road, to criticize and repudiate the reactionary bourgeois academic "authorities" and the ideology of the bourgeoisie and all other exploiting classes and to transform education, literature, and art and all other parts of the superstructure that do not correspond to the socialist economic base, so as to facilitate the consolidation and development of the socialist system.

2. The masses of the workers, peasants, soldiers, revolutionary intellectuals, and revolutionary cadres form the main force in this great cultural revolution. Large numbers of revolutionary young people, previously unknown, have become courageous and daring pathbreakers. They are vigorous in action and intelligent. Through the media of big-character posters and great debates, they argue things out, expose and criticize thoroughly, and launch resolute attacks on the open and hidden representatives of the bourgeoisie. In such a great revolutionary movement, it is hardly avoidable that they should show shortcomings of one kind or another, but their main revolutionary orientation has been correct from the beginning. This is the main current in the Great Proletarian Cultural Revolution. It is the main direction along which the Great Proletarian Cultural Revolution continues to advance.

Since the cultural revolution is a revolution, it inevitably meets with resistance. This resistance comes chiefly from those in authority who have wormed their way into the Party and are taking the capitalist road. It also comes from the old force of habit in society. At present, this resistance is still fairly strong and stubborn. However, the Great Proletarian Cultural Revolution is, after all, an irresistible general trend. There is abundant evidence that such resistance will crumble fast once the masses become fully aroused.

Because the resistance is fairly strong, there will be reversals and even repeated reversals in this struggle. There is no harm in this. It tempers the proletariat and other working people, and especially the younger generation, teaches them lessons and gives them experience, and helps them to understand that the revolutionary road is a zigzag one, and not plain sailing.

3. The outcome of this great cultural revolution will be determined by whether the Party leadership does or does not dare boldly to arouse the masses.

Currently, there are four different situations with regard to the leadership being given to the movement of cultural revolution by Party organizations at various levels:

(1) There is the situation in which the persons in charge of Party organizations stand in the van of the movement and dare to arouse the masses boldly. They put daring above everything else, they are dauntless Communist fighters and good pupils of Chairman Mao. They advocate the big-character posters and great debates. They encourage the masses to expose every kind of ghost and monster and also to criticize the shortcomings and errors in the work of the persons in charge. This correct kind of leadership is the result of putting proletarian politics in the forefront and Mao Tse-tung's thought in the lead.

(2) In many units, the persons in charge have a very poor understanding of the task of leadership in this great struggle, their leadership is far from being conscientious and effective, and they accordingly find themselves incompetent and in a weak position. They put fear above everything else, stick to outmoded ways and regulations, and are unwilling to break away from conventional prac-

tices and move ahead. They have been taken unawares by the new order of things, the revolutionary order of the masses, with the result that their leadership lags behind the situation, lags behind the masses.

(3) In some units, the persons in charge, who made mistakes of one kind or another in the past, are even more prone to put fear above everything else, being afraid that the masses will catch them out. Actually, if they make serious self-criticism and accept the criticism of the masses, the Party and the masses will make allowances for their mistakes. But if the persons in charge don't, they will continue to make mistakes and become obstacles to the mass movement.

(4) Some units are controlled by those who have wormed their way into the Party and are taking the capitalist road. Such persons in authority are extremely afraid of being exposed by the masses and therefore seek every possible pretext to suppress the mass movement. They resort to such tactics as shifting the targets for attack and turning black into white in an attempt to lead the movement astray. When they find themselves very isolated and no longer able to carry on as before, they resort still more to intrigues, stabbing people in the back, spreading rumors, and blurring the distinction between revolution and counterrevolution as much as they can, all for the purpose of attacking the revolutionaries.

What the Central Committee of the Party demands of the Party committees at all levels is that they persevere in giving correct leadership, put daring above everything else, boldly arouse the masses, change the state of weakness and incompetence where it exists, encourage those comrades who have made mistakes but are willing to correct them to cast off their mental burdens and join in the struggle, and dismiss from their leading posts all those in authority who are taking the capitalist road and so make possible the recapture of the leadership for the proletarian revolutionaries.

4. In the Great Proletarian Cultural Revolution, the only method is for the masses to liberate themselves, and any method of doing things on their behalf must not be used.

Trust the masses, rely on them, and respect their initiative. Cast out fear. Don't be afraid of disorder. Chairman Mao has often told us that revolution cannot be so very refined, so gentle, so temperate, kind, courteous, restrained, and magnanimous. Let the masses educate themselves in this great revolutionary movement and learn to distinguish between right and wrong and between correct and incorrect ways of doing things.

Make the fullest use of big-character posters and great debates to argue matters out, so that the masses can clarify the correct views, criticize the wrong views, and expose all the ghosts and monsters. In this way the masses will be able to raise their political consciousness in the course of the struggle, enhance their abilities and talents, distinguish right from wrong, and draw a clear line between the enemy and ourselves.

5. Who are our enemies? Who are our friends? This is a question of the first importance for the revolution and it is likewise a question of the first importance for the great cultural revolution.

Party leadership should be good at discovering the left and developing and strengthening the ranks of the left, and should firmly rely on the revolutionary left. During the movement this is the only way to isolate thoroughly the most reactionary rightists, win over the middle, and unite with the great majority, so that by the end of the movement we shall achieve the unity of more than 95 percent of the cadres and more than 95 percent of the masses.

Concentrate all forces to strike at the handful of ultra-reactionary bourgeois rightists and counterrevolutionary revisionists, and expose and criticize to the full their crimes against the Party, against socialism, and against

Mao Tse-tung's thought so as to isolate them to the maximum.

The main target of the present movement is those within the Party who are in authority and are taking the capitalist road.

Care should be taken to distinguish strictly between the anti-Party, antisocialist rightists and those who support the Party and socialism but have said or done something wrong or have written some bad articles or other works.

Care should be taken to distinguish strictly between the reactionary bourgeois scholar despots and "authorities" on the one hand and people who have the ordinary bourgeois academic ideas on the other.

6. A strict distinction must be made between the two different types of contradictions: those among the people and those between ourselves and the enemy. Contradictions among the people must not be made into contradictions between ourselves and the enemy; nor must contradictions between ourselves and the enemy be regarded as those among the people.

It is normal for the masses to hold different views. Contention between different views is unavoidable, necessary, and beneficial. In the course of normal and full debate, the masses will affirm what is right, correct what is wrong, and gradually reach unanimity.

The method to be used in debates is to present the facts, reason things out, and persuade through reasoning. Any method of forcing a minority holding different views to submit is impermissible. The minority should be protected, because sometimes the truth is with the minority. Even if the minority is wrong, they should still be allowed to argue their case and reserve their views.

When there is a debate, it should be conducted by reasoning, not by coercion or force.

In the course of debate, every revolutionary should be good at thinking things out for himself and should develop the Communist spirit of daring to think, daring to speak, and daring to act. On the premise that they have the same main orientation, revolutionary comrades should, for the sake of strengthening unity, avoid endless debate over side issues.

7. In certain schools, units, and work teams of the cultural revolution, some of the persons in charge have organized counterattacks against the masses who put up big-character posters against them. These people have even advanced such slogans as: opposition to the leaders of a unit or a work team means opposition to the Party's Central Committee, means opposition to the Party and socialism, means counterrevolution. In this way it is inevitable that their blows will fall on some really revolutionary activists. This is an error on matters of orientation, an error of line, and is absolutely impermissible.

A number of persons who suffer from serious ideological errors, and particularly some of the anti-Party and anti-socialist rightists, are taking advantage of certain shortcomings and mistakes in the mass movement to spread rumors and gossip, and engage in agitation, deliberately branding some of the masses as "counterrevolutionaries." It is necessary to beware of such "pickpockets" and expose their tricks in good time.

In the course of the movement, with the exception of cases of active counterrevolutionaries where there is clear evidence of crimes such as murder, arson, poisoning, sabotage, or theft of state secrets, which should be handled in accordance with the law, no measures should be taken against students at universities, colleges, middle schools, and primary schools because of problems that arise in the movement. To prevent the struggle from being diverted from its main objective, it is not allowed, whatever the pretext, to incite the masses to struggle against each other or the students to do likewise. Even proven rightists should be dealt with on the merits of each case at a later stage of the movement.

8. The cadres fall roughly into the following four categories:

(1) good;

(2) comparatively good;

(3) those who have made serious mistakes but have not become anti-Party, antisocialist rightists;

(4) the small number of anti-Party, antisocialist rightists.

In ordinary situations, the first two categories (good and comparatively good) are the great majority.

The anti-Party, antisocialist rightists must be fully exposed, hit hard, pulled down and completely discredited and their influence eliminated. At the same time, they should be given a way out so that they can turn over a new leaf.

9. Many new things have begun to emerge in the Great Proletarian Cultural Revolution. The cultural revolutionary groups, committees, and other organizational forms created by the masses in many schools and units are something new and of great historic importance.

These cultural revolutionary groups, committees, and congresses are excellent new forms of organization whereby under the leadership of the Communist Party the masses are educating themselves. They are an excellent bridge to keep our Party in close contact with the masses. They are organs of power of the proletarian cultural revolution.

The struggle of the proletariat against the old ideas, culture, customs, and habits left over from all the exploiting classes over thousands of years will necessarily take a very, very long time. Therefore the cultural revolutionary groups, committees, and congresses should not be temporary organizations but permanent, standing mass organizations. They are suitable not only for colleges, schools, and government and other organizations, but generally also for factories, mines, other enterprises, urban districts, and villages.

It is necessary to institute a system of general elections, like that of the Paris Commune, for electing members to the cultural revolutionary groups and committees and delegates to the cultural revolutionary congresses. The lists of candidates should be put forward by the revolutionary masses after full discussion, and the elections should be held after the masses have discussed the lists over and over again.

The masses are entitled at any time to criticize members of the cultural revolutionary groups and committees and delegates elected to the cultural revolutionary congresses. If these members or delegates prove incompetent, they can be replaced through election or recalled by the masses after discussion.

The cultural revolutionary groups, committees, and congresses in colleges and schools should consist mainly of representatives of the revolutionary students. At the same time, they should have a certain number of representatives of the revolutionary teaching staff and workers.

10. In the Great Proletarian Cultural Revolution a most important task is to transform the old educational system and the old principles and methods of teaching.

In this great cultural revolution, the phenomenon of our schools being dominated by bourgeois intellectuals must be completely changed.

In every kind of school we must apply thoroughly the policy advanced by Comrade Mao Tse-tung, of education serving proletarian politics and education being combined with productive labor, so as to enable those receiving an education to develop morally, intellectually, and physically and to become laborers with socialist consciousness and culture.

The period of schooling should be shortened. Courses should be fewer and better. The teaching material should be thoroughly transformed, in some cases beginning with simplifying complicated material. While their main task is to study, students should also learn other things. That is to say, in addition to their studies they should also learn industrial work, farming, and military affairs, and take part in the struggles of the cultural revolution as they occur to criticize the bourgeoisie.

11. In the course of the mass movement of the cultural revolution, the criticism of bourgeois and feudal ideology should be well combined with the dissemination of the proletarian world outlook and of Marxism-Leninism, Mao Tse-tung's thought.

Criticism should be organized of typical bourgeois representatives who have wormed their way into the Party and typical reactionary bourgeois academic "authorities," and this should include criticism of various kinds of reactionary views in philosophy, history, political economy, and education, in works and theories of literature and art, in theories of natural science, and in other fields.

Criticism of anyone by name in the press should be decided after discussion by the Party committee at the same level, and in some cases submitted to the Party committee at a higher level for approval.

12. As regards scientists, technicians, and ordinary members of working staffs, as long as they are patriotic, work energetically, are not against the Party and socialism, and maintain no illicit relations with any foreign country, we should in the present movement continue to apply the policy of "unity, criticism, unity." Special care should be taken of those scientists and scientific and technical personnel who have made contributions. Efforts should be made to help them gradually transform their world outlook and their style of work.

13. The cultural and educational units and leading organs of the Party and government in the large and medium cities are the points of concentration of the present proletarian cultural revolution.

The great cultural revolution has enriched the Socialist Education Movement in both city and countryside and raised it to a higher level. Efforts should be made to conduct these two movements in close combination. Arrangements to this effect may be made by various regions and departments in the light of the specific conditions.

The Socialist Education Movement now going on in the

countryside and in enterprises in the cities should not be upset where the original arrangements are appropriate and the movement is going well, but should continue in accordance with the original arrangements. However, the questions that are arising in the present Great Proletarian Cultural Revolution should be put to the masses for discussion at a proper time, so as to further foster vigorously proletarian ideology and eradicate bourgeois ideology.

In some places the Great Proletarian Cultural Revolution is being used as the focus in order to add momentum to the Socialist Education Movement and clean things up in the fields of politics, ideology, organization, and economy. This may be done where the local Party committee thinks it appropriate.

14. The aim of the Great Proletarian Cultural Revolution is to revolutionize people's ideology and as a consequence to achieve greater, faster, better, and more economical results in all fields of work. If the masses are fully aroused and proper arrangements are made, it is possible to carry on both the cultural revolution and production without one hampering the other, while guaranteeing high quality in all our work.

The Great Proletarian Cultural Revolution is a powerful motive force for the development of the social productive forces in our country. Any idea of counterposing the great cultural revolution against the development of production is incorrect.

15. In the armed forces, the cultural revolution and the Socialist Education Movement should be carried out in accordance with the instructions of the Military Commission of the Central Committee and the General Political Department of the People's Liberation Army.

16. In the Great Proletarian Cultural Revolution, it is imperative to hold aloft the great red banner of Mao Tse-tung's thought and put proletarian politics in command. The movement for the creative study and applica-

tion of Chairman Mao Tse-tung's works should be carried forward among the masses of the workers, peasants, and soldiers, the cadres and the intellectuals, and Mao Tse-tung's thought should be taken as the guide for action in the cultural revolution.

In this complex great cultural revolution, Party committees at all levels must study and apply Chairman Mao's works all the more conscientiously and in a creative way. In particular, they must study over and over again Chairman Mao's writings on the cultural revolution and on the Party's methods of leadership, such as *On the New Democracy, Talks at the Yenan Forum on Literature and Art, On the Correct Handling of Contradictions Among the People, Speech at the Chinese Communist Party's National Conference on Propaganda Work, Some Questions Concerning Methods of Leadership,* and *Methods of Work of Party Committees.*

Party committees at all levels must abide by the directions given by Chairman Mao over the years, namely that they should thoroughly apply the mass line of "from the masses and to the masses" and that they should be pupils before they become teachers. They should try to avoid being one-sided or narrow. They should foster materialist dialectics and oppose metaphysics and scholasticism.

The Great Proletarian Cultural Revolution is bound to achieve brilliant victory under the leadership of the Central Committee of the Party headed by Comrade Mao Tse-tung.

Constitution of the Communist Party of China

Adopted by the Ninth National Congress of the Communist Party of China on April 14, 1969

Chapter I   GENERAL PROGRAM

The Communist Party of China is the political party of the proletariat.

The basic program of the Communist Party of China is the complete overthrow of the bourgeoisie and all other exploiting classes, the establishment of the dictatorship of the proletariat in place of the dictatorship of the bourgeoisie, and the triumph of socialism over capitalism. The ultimate aim of the Party is the realization of communism.

The Communist Party of China is composed of the advanced elements of the proletariat; it is a vigorous vanguard organization leading the proletariat and the revolutionary masses in the fight against the class enemy.

The Communist Party of China takes Marxism-Leninism-Mao Tse-tung Thought as the theoretical basis guiding its thinking. Mao Tse-tung Thought is Marxism-Leninism of the era in which imperialism is heading for total collapse and socialism is advancing to world-wide victory.

For half a century now, in leading China's great struggle for accomplishing the new-democratic revolution, in leading her great struggle for socialist revolution and socialist construction, and in the great struggle of the contemporary international communist movement against imperialism, modern revisionism, and the reactionaries of various countries, Comrade Mao Tse-tung has integrated the universal truth of Marxism-Leninism with the concrete practice of revolution, inherited, defended, and developed Marxism-Leninism and has brought it to a higher and completely new stage.

Comrade Lin Piao has consistently held high the great red banner of Mao Tse-tung Thought and has most loyally and resolutely carried out and defended Comrade Mao Tse-tung's proletarian revolutionary line. Comrade Lin Piao is Comrade Mao Tse-tung's close comrade-in-arms and successor.

The Communist Party of China with Comrade Mao Tse-tung as its leader is a great, glorious, and correct Party and is the core of leadership of the Chinese people. The Party has been tempered through long years of class struggle for the seizure and consolidation of state power by armed force, it has strengthened itself and grown in the course of the struggle against both Right and "Left" opportunist lines, and it is valiantly advancing with supreme confidence along the road of socialist revolution and socialist construction.

Socialist society covers a fairly long historical period. Throughout this historical period, there are classes, class contradictions, and class struggle, there is the struggle between the socialist road and the capitalist road, there is the danger of capitalist restoration and there is the threat of subversion and aggression by imperialism and modern revisionism. These contradictions can be resolved only by depending on the Marxist theory of continued revolution and on practice under its guidance. Such is China's Great Proletarian Cultural Revolution, a great political revolution carried out under the conditions of socialism by the proletariat against the bourgeoisie and all other exploiting classes.

The whole Party must hold high the great red banner of Marxism-Leninism-Mao Tse-tung Thought and lead the hundreds of millions of the people of all the nationalities of our country in carrying on the three great revolutionary movements of class struggle, the struggle for production and scientific experiment, in strengthening and consolidating the dictatorship of the proletariat, and in building socialism independently and with the initiative in our own hands, through self-reliance and hard struggle and by going all out, aiming high and achieving greater, faster, better, and more economical results.

The Communist Party of China upholds proletarian internationalism; it firmly unites with the genuine Marxist-Leninist parties and groups the world over, unites with the proletariat, the oppressed people and nations of the whole world, and fights together with them to overthrow imperialism headed by the United States, modern revisionism with the Soviet revisionist renegade clique as its center, and the reactionaries of all countries, and to abolish the system of exploitation of man by man on the globe, so that all mankind will be emancipated.

Members of the Communist Party of China, who dedicate their lives to the struggle for communism, must be resolute, fear no sacrifice, and surmount every difficulty to win victory!

Chapter II   MEMBERSHIP

Article 1. Any Chinese worker, poor peasant, lower-middle peasant, revolutionary armyman, or any other revolutionary element who has reached the age of eighteen and who accepts the Constitution of the Party, joins a Party organization and works actively in it, carries out the Party's decisions, observes Party discipline, and pays membership dues may become a member of the Communist Party of China.

Article 2. Applicants for Party membership must go through the procedure for admission individually. An applicant must be recommended by two Party members, fill out an application form for Party membership, and be examined by a Party branch, which must seek the opinions of the broad masses inside and outside the Party. Application is subject to acceptance by the general membership meeting of the Party branch and approval by the next higher Party committee.

Article 3. Members of the Communist Party of China must:

(1) Study and apply Marxism-Leninism-Mao Tse-tung Thought in a living way;

(2) Work for the interests of the vast majority of the people of China and the world;

(3) Be able at uniting with the great majority, including those who have wrongly opposed them but are sincerely correcting their mistakes; however, special vigilance must be maintained against careerists, conspirators, and double-dealers so as to prevent such bad elements from usurping the leadership of the Party and the state at any level and guarantee that the leadership of the Party and the state always remains in the hands of Marxist revolutionaries;

(4) Consult with the masses when matters arise;

(5) Be bold in making criticism and self-criticism.

Article 4. When Party members violate Party discipline, the Party organizations at the levels concerned shall, within their functions and powers and on the merits of each case, take appropriate disciplinary measures—warning, serious warning, removal from posts in the Party, placing on probation within the Party, or expulsion from the Party.

The period for which a Party member is placed on

probation shall not exceed two years. During this period, he has no right to vote or elect or be elected.

A Party member who becomes politically apathetic and makes no change despite education should be persuaded to withdraw from the Party.

When a Party member asks to withdraw from the Party, the Party branch concerned shall, with the approval of its general membership meeting, remove his name from the Party rolls and report the matter to the next higher Party committee for the record. When necessary, this should be made public to the masses outside the Party.

Proven renegades, enemy agents, absolutely unrepentant persons in power taking the capitalist road, degenerates, and alien class elements must be cleared out of the Party and not be readmitted.

Chapter III
ORGANIZATIONAL PRINCIPLE OF THE PARTY

Article 5. The organizational principle of the Party is democratic centralism.

The leading bodies of the Party at all levels are elected through democratic consultation.

The whole Party must observe unified discipline: The individual is subordinate to the organization, the minority is subordinate to the majority, the lower level is subordinate to the higher level, and the entire Party is subordinate to the Central Committee.

Leading bodies of the Party at all levels shall regularly report on their work to congresses or general membership meetings, constantly listen to the opinions of the masses both inside and outside the Party and accept their supervision. Party members have the right to criticize Party organizations and leading members at all levels and make proposals to them. If a Party member holds different views with regard to the decisions or directives of the Party organizations, he is allowed to reserve his views and has the right to by-pass the immediate leadership and report directly to higher levels, up to and including the Central Committee and the Chairman of the Central Committee. It is essential to create a political situation in which there are both centralism and democracy, both discipline and freedom, both unity of will and personal ease of mind and liveliness.

The organs of the state power of the dictatorship of the proletariat, the People's Liberation Army, and the Communist Youth League and other revolutionary mass organizations, such as those of the workers, the poor and lower-middle peasants, and the Red Guards, must all accept the leadership of the Party.

Article 6. The highest leading body of the Party is the National Party Congress and, when it is not in session, the Central Committee elected by it. The leading bodies of Party organizations in the localities, in army units, and in various departments are the Party congresses or general membership meetings at their respective levels and the Party committees elected by them. Party congresses at all levels are convened by Party committees at their respective levels.

The convening of Party congresses in the localities and army units and their elected Party committee members are subject to approval by the higher Party organizations.

Article 7. Party committees at all levels shall set up their working bodies or dispatch their representative organs in accordance with the principles of unified leadership, close ties with the masses, and simple and efficient structure.

Chapter IV
CENTRAL ORGANIZATIONS OF THE PARTY

Article 8. The National Party Congress shall be convened every five years. Under special circumstances, it may be convened before its due date or postponed.

Article 9. The plenary session of the Central Committee

of the Party elects the Political Bureau of the Central Committee, the Standing Committee of the Political Bureau of the Central Committee, and the Chairman and Vice-Chairman of the Central Committee.

The plenary session of the Central Committee of the Party is convened by the Political Bureau of the Central Committee.

When the Central Committee is not in plenary session, the Political Bureau of the Central Committee and its Standing Committee exercise the functions and powers of the Central Committee.

Under the leadership of the Chairman, the Vice-Chairman, and the Standing Committee of the Political Bureau of the Central Committee, a number of necessary organs, which are compact and efficient, shall be set up to attend to the day-to-day work of the Party, the government, and the army in a centralized way.

Chapter V PARTY ORGANIZATIONS IN THE LOCALITIES AND THE ARMY UNITS

Article 10. Local Party congresses at the county level and upwards and Party congresses in the People's Liberation Army at the regimental level and upwards shall be convened every three years. Under special circumstances, they may be convened before their due date or postponed.

Party committees at all levels in the localities and the army units elect their standing committees, secretaries, and deputy secretaries.

Chapter VI PRIMARY ORGANIZATIONS OF THE PARTY

Article 11. In general, Party branches are formed in factories, mines, and other enterprises, people's communes, offices, schools, shops, neighborhoods, companies of the People's Liberation Army, and other primary units;

general Party branches or primary Party committees may also be set up where there is a relatively large membership or where the revolutionary struggle requires.

Primary Party organizations shall hold elections once a year. Under special circumstances, the election may take place before its due date or be postponed.

Article 12. Primary Party organizations must hold high the great red banner of Marxism-Leninism-Mao Tse-tung Thought, give prominence to proletarian politics, and develop the style of integrating theory with practice, maintaining close ties with the masses of the people, and practicing criticism and self-criticism. Their main tasks are:

(1) To lead the Party members and the broad revolutionary masses in studying and applying Marxism-Leninism-Mao Tse-tung Thought in a living way;

(2) To give constant education to the Party members and the broad revolutionary masses concerning class struggle and the struggle between the two lines and lead them in fighting resolutely against the class enemy;

(3) To propagate and carry out the policies of the Party, implement its decisions, and fulfill every task assigned by the Party and the state;

(4) To maintain close ties with the masses, constantly listen to their opinions and demands, and wage an active ideological struggle within the Party so as to keep Party life vigorous;

(5) To take in new Party members, enforce Party discipline, constantly consolidate the Party organizations, and get rid of the stale and take in the fresh so as to maintain the purity of the Party ranks.

Index

Index

Cambodia, 3–4, 11, 173, 175, 181, 234
Cancer, 53, 58
Canton, Trade Fair at, 9
Capital Hospital, 32
Capitalism and capitalists, 19, 84, 172, 179, 200, 203, 210, 221, 231, 239, 241–242
Captives, treatment of, 127, 174
Chang Hsueh-liang, 12
Chang Wei-shen, 55, 60–61
Chang Wen-t'ien, 78
Chekiang, 9, 150
Chen, Jerome, 66n.
Chen, William Y., 35–36, 39, 56
Ch'en Yi, 215
Ch'en Yung-kuei, 44–45, 146
Chiang Ch'ing, 86–87
Chiang Kai-shek, 11n., 49, 74, 85, 159, 172, 184, 192, 198–199, 202, 217–219, 222, 233
Ch'iao Kuan-hua, 69, 191
Childbirth, 33, 42
China, *see also* People's Republic; divisions of, as North China
  beautification of, 24
  and Britain, 230–231
  civil wars in, 7
  foreign policy of, 162–163, 176
  life in, 23–28
  minority nationalities in, 5, 203–204
  population of, 48–49, 156, 208, 213, 230–231
  Russia and, *see* Sino-Soviet relations
  size of, 137
  and the United Nations, 211–213
  United States and, 7, 10–12, 131, 159–160, 171–172, 179, 211–213, 215–219, 225
  and world relationships,
159–160, 162–163, 176, 224–225
Chinese army, 78–79, 90, 99, 108–109, 248; *see also* Army; People's Liberation Army
  as builder, 111–116
  and the people, 128–134
Chinese Communist Party, 4, 13–22, 65–67, 73, 76, 79, 83, 86–87, 99, 148–149, 157–158, 196, 221
  army and, 99–105, 133–134
  Central Committee, 72, 76, 78, 80, 85, 87–95, 146, 157, 170, 195, 238, 241, 244, 249, 254–256
  central organizations of, 255–256
  constitution of, 92, 158, 250–257
  and cultural revolution, 238–249
  membership in, 252–254
  Military Affairs Committee, 67
  organizational principle of, 254–255
  organizations of, in localities and army units, 256
  primary organizations of, 256–257
  program of, 250–252
  Propaganda Department, 80
Chou En-lai, 3, 7, 9, 14, 34, 45–46, 49–50, 69, 96, 99, 103, 134, 138, 192, 196
  descriptions of, 10, 153, 185–186, 224
  and Mao, 186–187
  and Nixon, 185, 187
  talks with, 153–163, 182–183, 218, 224–237
Chou Wen-chiang, General, 133
Chou Yang, 16, 85
Chu Shao-ch'ing, 112–114
Chu Ten, 99

About the Author

EDGAR SNOW, a native of Missouri, went to the Far East when he was twenty-two. He made his home in China for twelve years, studied the country and the language, and lectured at Yenching University in Peking, where he made friendships with students who are among China's leaders today. As a foreign correspondent in China, Burma, India, and Indochina he worked successively for the *Chicago Tribune, New York Sun, New York Herald Tribune,* and *London Daily Herald.* Then, as associate editor of the *Saturday Evening Post,* he reported wartime and postwar events in Asia and Europe, and became its widely quoted specialist on China, India, and the U.S.S.R. Edgar Snow was the author of eleven books, including *Red Star Over China, The Battle for Asia, People on Our Side, Red China Today: The Other Side of the River,* and *Journey to the Beginning.* He died in 1972.

VINTAGE POLITICAL SCIENCE
AND SOCIAL CRITICISM

VINTAGE BELLES—LETTRES

VINTAGE FICTION, POETRY, AND PLAYS

VINTAGE BIOGRAPHY AND AUTOBIOGRAPHY

VINTAGE WORKS OF SCIENCE
AND PSYCHOLOGY